ENDURANCE RUNNING

ENDURANCE RUNNING

NORMAN BROOK

British Amateur Athletic Board

THE CROWOOD PRESS

First published in 1987 by
THE CROWOOD PRESS LTD
Ramsbury, Marlborough
Wiltshire SN8 2HR

Paperback edition 1988

This impression 1992

British Library Cataloguing in Publication Data

Brook, Norman
  Endurance running.
  1. Running   2. Marathon running
  I. Title
  796.4'26   GV1061
  ISBN 0 946284 14 8 (HB)
      1 85223 125 4 (PB)

Dedicated to my parents, Duncan and Mavis

Acknowledgements

The author extends his thanks to all the coaches in the BAAB
Coaching Scheme and exercise physiologists who have contributed
to his understanding of endurance training theory and practice, and
to his wife, Claire, for her encouragement.

Cover photographs courtesy of Mark Shearman

Figs 1, 7, 64 and frontispiece by Alan Pascoe Associates; Figs 9, 20,
56, 58, 60, 63 and 65 by Wilfred Green Photography; Fig 53 by
Allan J. McCullough; Fig 54 by Bob Hamilton; Fig 61 by the Belfast
Telegraph; Fig 62 by K. Davis.

Diagrams by Ernie Williams and the author

Series Adviser David Bunker, Lecturer, Loughborough University of
Technology

Note Throughout this book, the pronouns 'he', 'him' and 'his' have
been used inclusively, and are intended to apply to both men and
women. It is important in sport, as elsewhere, that women and men
should have equal status and equal opportunities.

Typset by Acûté, Stroud, Glos.
Printed and bound in Great Britain
by Redwood Press Ltd, Melksham

Contents

Norman Brook was appointed National Athletics Coach to Northern Ireland in 1982 and Chief Coach for endurance events in 1985. He was born and educated in Scotland where he also taught as a secondary school teacher. In 1978 he returned to higher education to study Coaching Science at Dunfermline College of Physical Education (Edinburgh) and at Lakehead University (Canada).

Endurance running has become popular in recent years as a result of the increase in mass participation runs and the media's interest in athletes such as Cram, Coe and Ovett. To become successful as a runner, no matter what your level, you have to follow a training programme based on sound training principles. I have been fortunate in having a knowledgeable and practical coach who has set my training programme, but many of today's runners plan their own and they will find the advice given by Norman Brook helpful in plotting their success.

Tom McKean
European Championship Silver Medallist at 800m

It is my pleasure to write a foreword to this fine book by my colleague and friend, Norman Brook. As Chief Coach for endurance and as a student of 'sports science', he has committed considerable time and energy to the study of this sector of the sport. His enthusiasm for, and research into, the endurance events brings fresh sparkle to this, the most documented area of track and field athletics. The content includes all facets of the various endurance events and affords thoughtful coverage of special situations, such as young athletes and female athletes.

I believe that this publication will lead to more effective work in the endurance events in the long run — and in the short run!

Frank W. Dick
Director of Coaching
British Amateur Athletic Board

When I first started running as a junior girl in my local club, women were rarely seen training. Happily, this situation has now changed and it is common to see women out training on the roads. Competitive opportunities have also improved in recent years, with more local races for women and a wider range of events at international level.

In his book Norman Brook has devoted special attention to women, highlighting the physiological differences between the sexes and offering useful advice on training, making it essential reading for the coach of the female runner.

Liz Lynch
1986 Commonwealth Games 10,000m Gold Medallist
United Kingdom 10,000m record holder

Introduction

Running is such a natural activity that it is likely that men have always run against each other and that some of these challenges were tests of their powers of endurance. The first recorded endurance races date back to about 3800 BC when races of 3,200m were held in Egypt, running four repetitions between two pillars 800m apart. There were long distance runs in the ancient Olympic Games, which started in Greece in 776 BC and included an event called the *dolichos* which was run over a distance of around 5,000m.

When the modern Olympic Games were initiated in Athens in 1896, three endurance events were held: the 800m, 1,500m and marathon. The marathon was introduced to Baron de Coubertin's revival of the ancient Games, because the Frenchman, Michel Breal, had offered to donate a trophy to celebrate the legendary run of Pheidippides. According to Greek legend, Pheidippides, a soldier, ran the 35km from Marathon to Athens in 490 BC carrying news of the Greek victory over the invading Persians. He announced the victory to his Greek elders with the words 'Rejoice, we conquer' and then fell down dead. The actual distance of the marathon varied in the first few Olympic Games and it was only in 1924 that 26 miles 385 yards became accepted as the standard distance. This was the length of the marathon course used in the 1908 Games which were held in London. The race was to have been held over the 26 miles from Windsor Castle Grounds to the White City Stadium, but an extra 385 yards had to be added so that the race could finish in front of the Royal Box.

The 800m at the first Olympics was the metric equivalent of the half-mile, an event included in the AAA Championships which started in 1866. The mile equivalent should have been 1,600m, but it is thought that 1,500m was chosen as most tracks at that time were 500m long.

Cross-country running was included in three of the early Olympic Games (1912, 1920 and 1924) over a course of 8,000m to 10,000m in length. Also introduced in 1912 were 5,000m and 10,000m track events which still survive today, unlike the 3,000m team race which, along with the cross-country event, was dropped from the programme. The 3,000m steeplechase was introduced in 1920.

Women's endurance events are relatively new to the Olympic programme. The 800m was included when women's events were first introduced in 1928. As few women had trained for the race, many finished in a distressed state and this led to the event being dropped. It was 1960 before the 800m was reintroduced, and in 1972 the 1,500m was added. A women's 3,000m and marathon were held for the first time in 1984, and in 1988 it is intended that there should be a 10,000m.

OLYMPIC SUCCESS

British runners have enjoyed success in both the 800m and 1,500m races throughout the history of the modern Olympics. Alfred Tysoe (800m) and Charles Bennett

Introduction

(1,500m) started this tradition in the Paris Games of 1900. Since then Arnold Jackson (1912, 800m), Albert Hill (1920, 800m/ 1,500m double), Douglas Lowe (1924 and 1928, 800m), Thomas Hampson (1932, 800m), Steve Ovett (1980, 800m) and Sebastian Coe (1980 and 1984, 1,500m) have all taken titles.

In 1908 Alf Shrubb, the first great long distance runner of the twentieth century, wrote:

The Briton has a far greater stamina, as has been proved over and over again by our superiority in long distance races . . . There are not too many endurance events on the Olympic programme, but those there are should all be annexed by British representatives if only our men will make up their minds to do so.

Since 1908 Britain has produced many top class endurance athletes, yet to this date has still to produce an Olympic champion in the 5,000m, 10,000m or marathon. More success has been enjoyed in the 3,000m steeplechase, which Percy Hodge won in 1920 and in which Chris Brasher was the surprise victor in 1956, his first major win. In the women's events, only Anne Packer in the 800m in 1964 has ever won an Olympic title.

WORLD RECORDS

Throughout the twentieth century Britain has produced many of the world's best middle and long distance runners, although not all have been successful in major games. Alf Shrubb was the first of these great runners, producing nine world records between 1903 and 1904, his last four on the same day in November 1904 in the City of Glasgow. Shrubb was also the first runner or coach to put forward a training system. His system included running only twenty days each month and the use of long runs at a relaxed pace.

The most acclaimed performance by a middle distance runner in the twentieth century is still the first sub-4-minute mile by Roger Bannister. On 6 May 1954 in Oxford, Bannister ran a time of 3 minutes 59.4 seconds, a record that was to last for only one month, being improved by Australian, John Landy, to 3 minutes 57.8 seconds. Roger Bannister won the Empire Games and European titles, but never won an Olympic medal. He missed the 1948 games as he felt he lacked maturity for such an occasion and in 1952 he had to settle for fourth place.

A contemporary of Bannister was the marathon runner Jim Peters, who had the distinction of running four world bests over three years, 1952 to 1954. Unfortunately, he failed to finish in two major games, the 1952 Olympics and the 1954 Empire Games. It was in the latter that Peters shocked the sporting world when he collapsed with dehydration yards from the finish line and twenty minutes ahead of the next runner.

Another runner who was destined not to win a major games, but whose courageous front running caught the imagination of the public, was David Bedford. He dominated 5,000m and 10,000m running in late 1960s and early 1970s, breaking many records and earning a reputation as a runner with an incredible appetite for miles during training. Bedford was reputed to have covered 200 miles in one week's training. He broke the world record for 10,000m at the 1973 AAA Championships, running 27 minutes 30.8 seconds.

In 1982 David Moorcroft displayed

Fig 1   Steve Ovett, Olympic Champion 1986 and a former world record
holder at 1,500m and the mile.

Introduction

similar courage, front running a 5,000m in Oslo and breaking the world record by 5 seconds, running 13.00.41. Unlike David Bedford, Moorcroft had taken up 5,000m running after an accomplished career as a 1,500m runner and was known to have a good sprint finish. His proven ability either to run from the front or to wait for a sprint finish made him the favourite to win the 1984 Olympic title. However, fate was not on Moorcroft's side and he was plagued with illness and injury in the two years between his world record and the Olympics, and although he made the final he was not to feature in the challenge for medals.

Three British athletes who dominated records and major championships in the early 1980s were Steve Ovett, Sebastian Coe and Steve Cram. Sebastian Coe started the British record breaking spree in 1979 when he captured the world records for the 800m, 1,500m and mile. The next year, 1980, Steve Ovett broke Coe's 1,500m and mile records, the 1,500m on two occasions. Sebastian Coe improved his 800m record in 1981 and regained the mile record, lost it to Ovett and then captured it for a second time that year. In 1983 the South African born Sydney Maree, who had taken American citizenship, set a new world record at 1,500m. However, Ovett responded with another record to keep all three records British at the end of that year. Steve Cram entered the record books in 1985 when he broke the 1,500m and mile records, but he didn't manage to keep the 1,500m which was improved later that year by Said Aouita.

1 The Physiology of Endurance Running

Running, like all other forms of movement, is made possible by the action of our muscles. Our muscles move our legs and arms in the running action by alternately contracting and relaxing. Inside each muscle there are muscle fibres, each one so thin that it can't be seen but long enough that it runs the full length of the muscle. These muscle fibres shorten along their lengths to contract the muscles and return to their normal lengths when the muscle relaxes. Every time a muscle fibre contracts, it uses energy which comes in the form of a substance called adenosine triphosphate (ATP).

THE ENERGY SYSTEMS

Adenosine triphosphate (ATP), the energy source which our muscles need, is a molecule consisting of an adenosine atom surrounded by three phosphate atoms. When the muscle fibres shorten along their lengths, ATP is used and as a result it loses one of its phosphate atoms and changes into another substance called adenosine diphosphate (ADP).

$$A - P \begin{array}{c} - P \\ - P \end{array} \xrightarrow{\text{'muscle contraction'}} A - P \begin{array}{c} \\ - P \end{array} + P$$

Without ATP the muscle fibres cannot shorten and movement cannot occur. To be able to run, therefore, our muscles need a constant supply of ATP. The aim of all endurance training is to ensure that our muscles have an adequate supply of energy in the form of ATP.

Energy in the form of ATP is provided through one of the following three energy systems:

1. Alactic – anaerobic energy system. (Phosphate stores; no lactic acid produced; no oxygen required.)
2. Lactic – anaerobic energy system. (Carbohydrate as fuel; lactic acid produced; no oxygen available.)
3. Aerobic energy system. (Carbohydrate and fat as fuel; no lactic acid produced; oxygen present.)

Alactic Anaerobic System

There is a small store of ATP contained within our muscles which would last about four seconds if we exercised as hard as we could. Any exercise which lasts more than four seconds requires fresh ATP to be found from one of the energy systems. The most immediate source of new ATP is found within the muscles' store of other phosphates, in a substance called creatine phosphate (CP). The ADP created when an ATP loses one of its phosphates combines with the CP to reconvert itself to ATP. It does this by borrowing one of the CP's phosphates.

$$\begin{matrix} & -P & & & -P \\ A & -P & + & C-P & \longrightarrow & A-P & + & C \\ & & & & & & & -P \end{matrix}$$

This method of producing ATP is also short-lived, as the muscles' store of creatine phosphate is limited – it is only three to four times the size of the ATP store and therefore lasts around twelve seconds.

To produce more ATP the muscles will now have to break down one of two fuels available in the body, either carbohydrate or fats. Carbohydrate can be broken down to produce ATP either with oxygen present, referred to as aerobic metabolism (aerobic means with oxygen), or without oxygen present, referred to as anaerobic metabolism (anaerobic means without oxygen). Fats, on the other hand, can only be broken down by the aerobic process.

Aerobic System

Provided there is an adequate supply of oxygen to the working muscles, carbohydrate in the form of glycogen and fats in the form of free fatty acids can be metabolised to produce ATP. With the encouragement of oxidative enzymes (organic catalysts which release and transfer energy) these two fuels are reduced to carbon dioxide and water. In the process they produce a number of ATP molecules.

Carbohydrate, available in the muscle as glycogen, is first of all converted to pyruvic acid in a process known as glycolysis producing three ATP molecules. The pyruvic acid is then taken up by cells within the muscles called mitochondria. The oxygen in the muscles is also taken up by these cells, which are often referred to as the 'engine rooms' of the muscle. In the

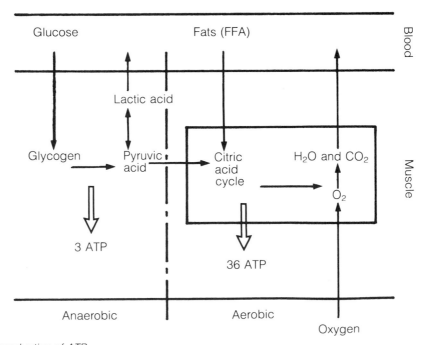

Fig 2   The production of ATP.

mitochondria, the pyruvic acid and oxygen are converted to carbon dioxide and water in a process which produces another 36 ATP molecules. The total number of ATP molecules produced by the aerobic metabolism of a unit of carbohydrate is 39.

Fats are available in the muscle as free fatty acids and they too, like the pyruvic acid, can be taken up by the mitochondria. Just as the pyruvic acid combines with the oxygen to produce 36 ATP molecules, so do the free fatty acids. The oxidation of fats produces 36 ATP as compared to the 39 produced when the fuel is carbohydrate. This explains why 12 per cent more oxygen is used to produce the same amount of energy from fats as from carbohydrate. Although fats are not as rich an energy source as carbohydrate, they have the advantage of being an almost inexhaustible store when compared to that of carbohydrate, which is only large enough to supply energy for approximately 100 minutes of marathon type running.

Lactic Anaerobic System

When there is insufficient oxygen available in the muscle to meet all of the energy demands through the aerobic system, energy can be made available through the anaerobic metabolism of carbohydrate. The muscle glycogen is converted to pyruvic acid through glycolysis (described above). As there is no oxygen available to combine with the pyruvic acid, there is no point in the mitochondria taking it up. The pyruvic acid is therefore converted to lactic acid. Unlike the waste products of aerobic metabolism which are easily dispersed, lactic acid has to wait until oxygen becomes available at a later stage to allow it to be reconverted to pyruvate or even glycogen. Until that happens, the lactic

acid which accumulates in the muscle and spills over into the bloodstream has a negative influence on performance.

The lactic acid which remains within the muscle inhibits the enzymes which enable glycogen to be converted to energy anaerobically and also inhibits the muscles from contracting. If too much lactate is allowed to build up in the muscle, the athlete will eventually be forced to cease running or at least slow down. From this viewpoint the production of lactic acid may be viewed as a negative limiting factor. However, for short distances such as 400m and 800m large amounts of energy need to be made available quickly to allow these distances to be run at speed. Although the anaerobic conversion of carbohydrate does not yield much energy for each unit used, the rate at which energy is produced far exceeds the speed of aerobic energy production. From this viewpoint the ability to produce lactic acid enhances performance in some running events.

Proportional Contribution
(Figs 3 & 4)

The proportion of energy contributed by each of the three energy systems is related to the speed of running. The faster a person runs, the greater the energy required. So when an athlete sprints over 100m he needs a large amount of energy which must be delivered quickly. The alactic anaerobic energy system can provide energy quickly in relatively large amounts, but the store is exhausted within a few seconds. The person running 400m or 800m also needs a lot of energy quickly, not as much as the 100m sprinter but certainly more than can be supplied by the aerobic energy system. As the energy from the alactic anaerobic system starts to

The Physiology of Endurance Running

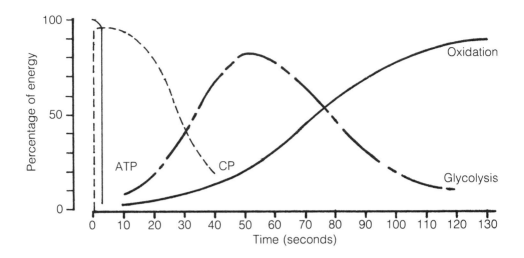

Fig 3   Proportional contribution of energy systems (Keul, 1973).

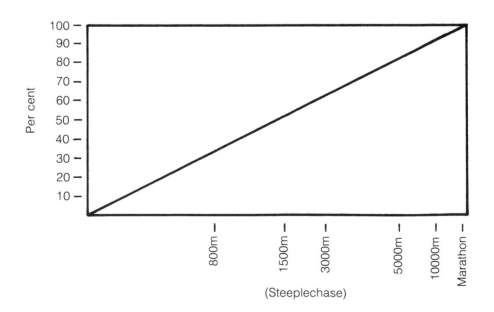

Fig 4   Aerobic/anaerobic contribution to energy requirements of athletic
endurance events.

become depleted after a few seconds, the 400m or 800m runner has to rely on the lactic anaerobic system as the major contributor of energy.

It should not be assumed that the three energy systems work independently of each other, with one being recruited as another becomes exhausted. This is not the case, as all three systems are contributing some ATP to meet the energy demands of running right from the start of activity. It is the duration and intensity of running which determine which of the three systems is most important.

Oxygen Transport System
(*Figs 5 & 6*)

The longer the duration of an event, the more important the aerobic system is in providing energy. In distances over a mile, the aerobic system provides most of the energy and is therefore the most important system to train. Even in events of less than a mile, such as the 800m and 1,500m, aerobic endurance is important, as a well-developed aerobic system will hold back the use of anaerobic energy.

If energy is to be provided by the aerobic system, a constant supply of oxygen has to be made available to the mitochondria. The oxygen needed is contained in the air that we breathe into our lungs. Air passes down the windpipe which divides into two branches, each leading into the two moist bags forming the lungs. Each branch further divides into smaller and smaller branches, eventually ending in tiny thin walled sacs called alveoli. Each of these sacs is surrounded by a basketwork of very fine blood vessels known as capillaries. It is in the alveoli that oxygen is taken out of the air and passed through its thin walls into the bloodstream. As oxygen passes

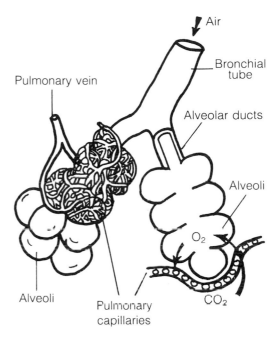

Fig 5   The alveoli and pulmonary capillaries.

into the blood, carbon dioxide is passed out of the bloodstream into the lungs for expiration. At rest, we breathe about twelve times per minute, but when running breathing rates increase to help take in more oxygen.

The blood which passes through the capillaries surrounding the alveoli is forced round the pulmonary (lung) circulatory system by the pumping action of the heart. The heart is divided into halves, which are separated by a thick muscular wall. In each side of the heart there is an upper and a lower chamber, the top one is called the atrium and the bottom one the ventricle. Between the atrium and the ventricle there is a valve which ensures that when the heart muscles contract, blood can only pass in one direction. Blood from the body's general or systemic circulatory system enters the right atrium depleted of

15

oxygen. The blood in the right atrium is pushed down into the right ventricle and in turn is forced round the pulmonary system as the heart contracts and squeezes blood out of the right ventricle. As the blood passes over the lungs, carbon dioxide is off-loaded and fresh supplies of oxygen are collected. The blood then re-enters the heart through the left atrium and passes to the left ventricle before being pumped round the body's systemic circulatory system.

The greater the volume of blood that can be passed round the systemic circulation in a given time, the more oxygen that is available to the mitochondria. The amount of blood pumped round the body by the heart each minute is known as the cardiac output. The cardiac output is the volume of blood which is pumped out each time the heart contracts multiplied by the heart rate:

Cardiac output = stroke volume × heart rate

Like other muscles the heart can be trained, making it stronger and able to increase the volume of blood it forces out with each beat. As a result of this increase, the rate at which the heart beats at rest and at set work loads falls. A greater volume of blood is now being circulated at a set heart rate supplying more oxygen to the muscles. As the oxygen demands at rest and at set loads do not rise, a lower heart rate will supply the oxygen needed.

Oxygen is carried in the blood by haemoglobin which is contained within the red blood cells. In the average male the haemoglobin concentration is 15.8g per 100ml of blood, while females have 13.7g per 100ml. The haemoglobin hold on to the oxygen until they reach the muscles through another fine network of capillaries. These capillaries spread throughout the muscles making it possible for the myoglobin contained in the muscle cells to attract oxygen away from the haemoglobin in the bloodstream. The oxygen attracted from the bloodstream is used in the mitochondria to oxidise fuel. The waste product of that chemical reaction, carbon dioxide, is deposited in the bloodstream allowing it to be carried via the heart to the lungs.

Maximal Oxygen Uptake

There is a limit to the amount of oxygen that can be transported to and utilised by the muscles. The amount of oxygen being used can be assessed with specialised equipment which measures the amount of oxygen breathed in and compares this with

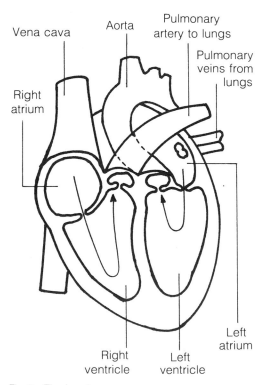

Fig 6   The heart.

Fig 7   Zola Budd's success over a range of middle-distance events
suggests that she has a high maximum oxygen uptake value.

the amount breathed out. The difference between the two is the oxygen utilised and this is referred to as the oxygen uptake. The maximum amount of oxygen the body can utilise is the maximal oxygen uptake (VO_2max). An individual's VO_2max is recorded as the amount of oxygen measured in litres utilised in one minute (1/min). One person, for example, may be capable of using a maximum of 3.5 litres of oxygen per minute. To allow comparisons to be made between individuals, this absolute value is often divided by bodyweight to give a relative score expressed in millilitres of oxygen utilised per minute per kilogram of bodyweight (ml/min/kg). This measure is commonly used to assess levels of aerobic fitness and to predict endurance performance. There is a considerable variation in VO_2max scores in the population with age and sex. The average range of scores for a male aged 20 to 29 would lie between 44–51ml/kg/min, while the average female of the same age would score between 35–43ml/kg/min. The elite male runner of similar age could expect to have a VO_2max score in the 70s or low 80s, while the top female runners in this age group would score in the 60s or low 70s.

TRAINING THRESHOLDS

Aerobic Threshold

If adaptations to training are to occur, the body has to be stressed. For changes to take place as a result of endurance training, the work-load has to push the individual beyond his aerobic training threshold. If the training load is of an intensity which doesn't reach the aerobic threshold, it will have no effect. The aerobic threshold can be expressed as a

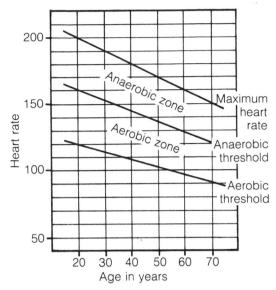

Fig 8 Aerobic and anaerobic training zones.

percentage of the person's maximal oxygen uptake or as a heart rate which correlates with this percentage. As the intensity of exercise increases, so too does the heart rate, making it a useful control of the training intensity. Karvonen has suggested the following formula to estimate the aerobic training threshold:

Heart rate = 70% × (max h.r. − resting h.r.) + resting h.r.
Maximum h.r. = 220 − your age

Anaerobic Threshold

As the speed of running increases and before maximal oxygen uptake has been reached, a second training threshold – the anaerobic threshold – is encountered. When running, the anaerobic threshold is marked by an increase in breathing rate and running effort. This is caused by the partial buffering or neutralising of rising blood lactic acid, which is the by-product of anaerobic work. Even though at this intensity most energy is being provided by the aerobic energy system, a gradually rising amount of energy is provided anaerobically. Bicarbonate present in the bloodstream reacts with the lactic acid caused by this anaerobic work producing carbon dioxide, which is a potent stimulator of respiration. Runners will recognise this situation: they are out running in a group at a steady pace conversing easily, one of their number increases the pace slightly, the runners start working harder, their breathing rate increases and their conversation ceases. The end of conversation indicates that the runners have crossed the anaerobic threshold. This has been called the conversational index, and athletes can use it to monitor the intensity of training runs.

The anaerobic threshold can be measured in the exercise physiology laboratory and can range from 50 per cent VO_2max in the untrained person to around 80 per cent in the highly trained athlete. Between an individual's aerobic threshold and anaerobic threshold lies his aerobic training zone, and between his anaerobic threshold and his maximal heart rate is the anaerobic training zone. When training within the aerobic zone, most energy can be provided by the aerobic energy system. This is not the case when the intensity increases and moves into the anaerobic training zone. There is then a shortage of oxygen in the muscle, so an increasing amount of energy has to be provided by the lactic anaerobic system.

Lactic Acid

The normal amount of lactic acid circulating in the blood varies between individuals, but is about 1–2 mmol/L (millimoles of lactate per litre of blood). In low intensity exercise, where energy needs can be met aerobically, there will be no significant increase in this level. In medium intensity exercise, such as a 20–30 minute run, lactic acid concentrations will rise 1.5–2 times, producing a figure of approximately 4 mmol/L. This figure corresponds to the anaerobic threshold. In high intensity exercise of 45 seconds to 2 minutes duration lactate levels can reach as high as 25 mmol/L which is 15–20 times resting values.

The optimal stimulus to produce an endurance training effect is thought to be a steady state value of around 4 mmol/L, the anaerobic threshold, although this can range in individuals from 2–7.5 mmol/L. This would be the highest exercise intensity that could be maintained over a period of 20–30 minutes without a progressive increase in lactic acid concentration occurring.

Lactic acid can be measured by medical staff using simple finger-prick blood samples and rapid automated lactate analysers. These can be taken at the track-side, providing a testing service which allows for the control and monitoring of both aerobic and anaerobic training sessions. This equipment is easy to use and extremely reliable, but it is expensive and must be used by trained medical staff.

In the exercise physiology lab, the physiologist can provide useful advice using blood lactate in addition to oxygen uptake analysis. In order to produce VO_2max or anaerobic threshold scores in the lab, athletes used to have to undertake an incremental run on the treadmill. This test would be a maximal test which was both physically and mentally demanding. The information from such a test was useful and if repeated over a period of time enabled training adaptations to be observed. However, the information gained from lactate tests has been shown to be more accurate in predicting performance and is less demanding of the athlete. The athlete can run a steady state for about 4–7 minutes and then a blood sample can be taken. There is no need to go through the progression of increasing work-loads nor is there any need to endure the discomfort of wearing the oxygen uptake equipment. It has always been difficult to observe improvements in VO_2max in trained athletes, but this is not the case with lactate values. Lactate tests are more sensitive measures of adaptation to endurance training than VO_2max estimation.

Adaptation to Training

The purpose of endurance training is to encourage physiological changes to take place which improve the runner's ability to produce and utilise energy. Changes to the alactic energy system will result from an increase in the phospogen stores of adenosine triphosphate and creatine phosphate. Training of a very short duration such as flat-out sprinting with a long recovery will promote these changes. Adaptations to the alactic anaerobic energy system are of more importance to power and speed athletes than they are to the endurance runner who has to keep working over extended periods of time.

Lactic anaerobic training will increase the muscles' ability to produce and tolerate lactic acid, in turn enhancing performance in shorter endurance events. Training increases anaerobic enzyme activity and the lactic acid buffers of bicarbonate and blood protein. It will also increase the muscles' ability to 'pump-out' lactic acid into the bloodstream. Training which

features intermittent runs of a relatively short duration but high intensity and which creates increases in lactate concentration of approximately 5 times the resting value will promote these training effects. As a high lactic acid concentration will detract from performance ability (when quality is required as it is in repetitions for speed endurance) then sufficient time must be given to allow lactate levels to fall to around 4–6mmol/L. Twenty minutes would seem to be an optimal period of time to allow lactate levels to fall. The recovery period, however, obviously depends on how intense the previous bout of exercise was and on how much lactate was accumulated. It is also accepted nowadays that active recovery leads to a quicker decrease in lactate levels than passive recovery. This has led to athletes 'warming down' after anaerobic repetition sessions in order to remove some of the accumulated lactate. There is, however, a body of opinion that rejects 'warming down' in order to oblige the system to build up the lactic acid buffers.

Adaptations to aerobic training improve the runner's ability both to transport oxygen to the working muscle and to utilise the oxygen that is made available. Training improves the cardiac output by increasing the amount of blood that can be pumped from the heart with each beat. A training effect can then be observed by recording the resting heart rate each morning. Total blood volume increases in response to training and the blood becomes less viscous, enabling it to flow more easily. The number of red blood cells and the total volume of haemoglobin also increases, but not necessarily in proportion to the total blood volume. Some tests which measure the concentration of haemoglobin will therefore show an apparent fall in haemoglobin scores in trained athletes suggest-

Fig 9   The marathon runner's high mileage, run at relatively low intensities, develops the ability to liberate fats as a source of energy.

ing that they are anaemic, when in fact they have more haemoglobin available.

The small blood vessels called capillaries, which spread throughout the working muscles, increase in number making the total surface area where blood is next to the muscle tissue greater. This makes more oxygen available within the muscle. The myoglobin, which take the oxygen from the bloodstream and pass it on to the mitochondria, increase in number with training. The mitochondria not only increase in number, but individual cells increase in size. The aerobic enzyme activity within the mitochondria also increases with training. These adaptations make it possible to liberate more energy aerobically.

Extensive aerobic training is thought to be capable of changing the characteristics of some types of muscle fibres. Some groups of muscle fibres are suited to slow aerobic work and are called slow twitch, oxidative or red fibres. Others are more suited to anaerobic work and are called fast twitch, glycolitic or white muscle fibres. The oxidative fibres have a good supply of blood, hence the term red fibres. The white fibres do not need a good supply of blood as they work anaerobically and therefore do not require oxygen. It is understood that in marathon type training some white fibres can, over a period of time, be converted to work as red fibres.

Aerobic training will either lead to improvements in the runner's maximal oxygen uptake and his ability to hold back the onset of lactic acid, or will increase the percentage of his VO_2max at which he can comfortably run over a long period of time. Aerobic training of a low intensity over prolonged periods of time will also increase fat mobilisation and spare carbohydrate, an important consideration in long distance events such as the marathon.

2 Endurance Training Methods

Specific training for all running events involves running sessions organised in one of three forms:

1. Intermittent – periods of running interspersed with periods of rest.
2. Continuous – a continuous run completed at a steady pace.
3. Mixed pace – a continuous run completed at a varying pace.

INTERMITTENT TRAINING

Intermittent training involves repeated runs interspersed with periods of rest. Rest periods can be active, where the runner jogs between runs, or can be passive, where the runner sits down between runs. This type of training is more commonly known as interval or repetition running – terms which can be confusing, as not all intermittent training sessions promote the same training effect. A set of 200m runs could be aimed at developing anaerobic endurance capacity, while a set of 1,500m runs might be aimed at developing aerobic power. Both sessions are intermittent training and could easily be referred to as either interval or repetition running, even though each session would have an entirely different training effect. One session could have an anaerobic training effect, while another could be aerobic and a third could have a mixed effect, partly aerobic and partly anaerobic. In order to avoid confusion over the aims of particular sessions, intermittent training aimed at developing the anaerobic systems is referred to as repetition running and that aimed at developing the aerobic system as interval running. Despite making this distinction between the two types of running, there will be some overlap between longer repetition sessions and shorter interval sessions, where there will be a mixed training effect.

There are a number of variables which can be altered in intermittent training to create different training loads:

1. The distance or duration of each repetition.
2. The speed (intensity) of each repetition.
3. The total number of repetitions and sets.
4. The recovery period.
5. The type of recovery – active versus passive.
6. The terrain over which each repetition is run.

These variables can be altered to create a wide range of training effects. One session of 200m runs, for example, could be performed as 2 × 4 × 200m with 30 second recovery and a 10 minute rest at 90 per cent effort. Another session using 200m repetitions might take the form of 12 × 200m with a 90 second recovery at 75 per cent effort. The first session would lead to higher concentrations of lactate than the second and would therefore have a different training effect.

Anaerobic Repetitions

Intermittent training to develop anaerobic endurance can be grouped into three main categories which correspond to the notion that anaerobic endurance can be classified as short, medium and long term:

Short Term	Medium Term	Long Term
0–25 secs	25–60 secs	60–120 secs
up to 200m	200–400m	400–800m

The three types of anaerobic intervals are:

1. *Speed work* Runs over distances up to 60m at maximum speed to develop pure speed or extended fast runs over distances from 60m to 150m to develop speed endurance. In both types of session allow adequate recovery periods between runs.
2. *Short duration/short recovery work* Repetitions of 100m to 400m duration with an effort:recovery ratio of around 1:1. Quality of each run should be maintained and if necessary sessions can be arranged in sets to allow recovery.
3. *Long duration/long recovery work* Repetitions of 400m to 1,000m duration with recovery periods of up to 10 minutes between sets. Quality of effort should remain high and should be maintained throughout the training session.

Training to develop speed should be conducted at a pace close to the runner's best for the distance. The key to successful anaerobic training is to keep the quality of runs high. Repetitions should not be allowed to fall below 85 to 90 per cent of the runner's best time for the distance. This type of anaerobic training is sometimes

referred to as speed or specific endurance, and it is essential that speed is maintained throughout the session. If the quality falls below 85 per cent during a speed endurance session there is little point in continuing the session. *Fig 10* provides an easy way of calculating training times based on the training intensity.

Aerobic Intervals

Aerobic endurance is also categorised as short, medium or long term:

Short Term	Medium Term	Long Term
2–8 mins	8–30 mins	30 mins +
800–3,000m	3,000–10,000m	10,000m +

Short term aerobic endurance is usually organised as interval training, as it would not be possible to continue high intensity aerobic work for longer without the periods of recovery. There are two types of aerobic interval session: extensive interval work and Gerschler Interval work.

Extensive Interval Work

Distances of 800m to 3,000m are run using recovery periods which are kept relatively short and, in fact, may be shortened as fitness improves. If work intervals last between 2 to 10 minutes, recovery times will range between 1 to 5 minutes. With extensive interval work the runner trains above the anaerobic threshold, with the muscles' oxygen requirements not being fully met and a small amount of energy being provided anaerobically. The shortage of oxygen within the muscle encourages improvement in maximal oxygen uptake.

High intensity aerobic running is more likely to develop the neurological pattern of muscle fibre recruitment used during races as training speeds are closely related to racing speed. As there is selective recruitment of muscle fibres at different speeds, low intensity running will not prepare the muscle fibres recruited during racing to meet the high rate of energy demands placed on them. The advantage of high intensity aerobic training is that it more accurately simulates the rate of energy expenditure and muscle fibre recruitment required during competition.

Gerschler Interval Work

Shorter distances of about 200m to 400m are run with a large number of repetitions, for example 20 × 200m, and using short recovery periods ranging from 2 minutes to 30 seconds. This type of interval training is thought to provide a strong stimulus to the heart during the recovery period, when the heart rate should fall from around 170–180 beats per minute down to around 120 130. These intervals also encourage a running pace more in tune with that used in competition and develop a sense of pace judgement.

CONTINUOUS TRAINING

Medium and long term aerobic work both involve training of a continuous nature. The intensity of these runs decreases as the duration of the runs increases. Continuous training is divided into two main types: medium steady runs or long slow runs.

Medium Steady Runs

Continuous runs over distances of around two to six miles form the backbone of all endurance runners' training programmes.

Most runners include five or six of these runs in their weekly programmes. This type of running has to be conducted at an intensity which corresponds to the runner's anaerobic threshold.

Long Slow Runs

These steady state runs last in duration from 30 minutes up to several hours. They are conducted at intensities which lie below the anaerobic threshold in the aerobic training zone. Such training develops the oxygen transport system and the runner's ability to perform prolonged activity at a high percentage of maximum oxygen uptake. The easy pace and the extended distance of these runs condition the runner to resist the fatigue of the race without straining the adaptation process. These long runs are important to the long distance athletes, such as the marathon runner, as they increase ability to utilise fats.

MIXED PACE TRAINING

It is possible to make continuous runs more stressful by varying the pace during the run and/or the terrain being covered. Hills can be included to stress the runner and take him closer to his VO_2 max. The fast and hard stages of the run force the runner to work close to the VO_2 max and induce a shortage of oxygen in the working muscles. This oxygen debt is repaid during the less stressful stages of the run. The periods during these runs when there is a shortage of oxygen encourage adaptation of the aerobic system. The common name given to this type of training is the Swedish for speed play – *fartlek*. Two types of fartlek are:

Endurance Training Methods

BEST TIME	TRAINING INTENSITY								
	60%	65%	70%	75%	80%	85%	90%	95%	98%
15"	25"	23"	21"4	20"	18"7	17"6	16"6	15"7	15"3
15"5	25"6	23"8	22"1	20"6	19"3	18"2	17"2	16"3	15"8
16"	26"6	24"6	22"8	21"3	20"	18"8	17"7	16"8	16"3
16"5	27"5	25"3	23"5	22"	20"6	19"4	18"3	17"3	16"8
17"	28"3	26"1	24"2	22"5	21"2	20"	18"8	17"8	17"3
17"5	29"1	26"9	25"	23"3	21"8	20"5	19"4	18"4	17"9
18"	30"	27"6	25"7	24"	22"5	21"1	20"	18"9	18"4
18"5	30"3	28"4	26"4	24"6	23"1	21"7	20"5	19"4	18"9
19"	31"6	29"2	27"4	25"3	23"7	22"3	21"1	20"	19"4
19"5	32"5	29"9	27"8	26"	24"3	22"9	21"6	20"5	19"9
20"	33"3	30"7	28"5	26"6	25"	23"5	22"2	21"	20"4
20"5	34"1	31"5	29"2	27"3	25"6	24"1	22"7	21"5	20"9
21"	35"	32"2	30"	28"	26"2	24"7	23"3	22"1	21"4
21"5	35"8	33"	30"7	28"6	26"8	25"2	23"8	22"6	21"9
22"	36"6	33"9	31"4	29"3	27"5	25"8	24"4	23"1	22"4
22"5	37"5	34"5	32"1	30"	28"1	26"4	25"	23"6	23"
23"	38"3	35"3	32"8	30"6	28"7	27"	25"5	24"2	23"5
23"5	39"4	36"1	33"5	31"5	29"3	27"6	26"1	24"7	24"
24"	40"	36"9	34"2	32"	30"	28"2	26"6	25"2	24"5
24"5	40"8	37"6	35"	32"6	30"6	28"8	27"2	25"7	25"
25"	41"6	38"4	35"7	33"3	31"2	29"4	27"7	26"3	25"5
25"5	42"5	39"2	36"4	34"	31"8	30"	28"3	26"8	26"
26"	43"3	40"	37"1	34"6	32"5	30"5	28"8	27"3	26"5
26"5	44"1	40"7	37"8	35"3	33"1	31"1	29"4	27"8	27"
27"	45"	41"5	38"5	36"	33"7	31"7	30"	28"4	27"5
27"5	45"6	42"3	39"2	36"6	34"3	32"3	30"5	28"9	28"1
28"	46"6	43"1	40"	37"3	35"	32"9	31"1	29"4	28"6
28"5	47"5	43"8	40"7	38"	35"6	33"5	31"6	30"	29"1
29"	48"3	44"6	41"4	38"6	36"2	34"1	32"2	30"5	29"6
29"5	49"1	45"4	42"1	39"3	36"8	34"7	32"7	31"	30"1
30"	50"	46"2	42"8	40"	37"5	35"2	33"3	31"5	30"6
30"5	50"8	46"9	43"5	40"6	38"1	35"8	33"8	32"1	31"1
31"	51"6	47"6	44"2	41"3	38"7	36"4	34"4	32"6	31"6
31"5	52"5	48"4	45"	42"	39"3	37"	35"	33"1	32"1
32"	53"3	49"2	45"7	42"6	40"	37"5	35"5	33"5	32"6
32"5	54"1	49"8	46"4	43"3	40"6	38"2	36"1	34"4	33"2
33"	55"	50"7	47"1	44"	41"2	38"8	36"6	34"7	33"7
33"5	55"3	51"5	47"8	44"6	41"8	39"4	37"2	35"2	34"2
34"	56"6	52"3	48"5	45"3	42"5	40"	37"7	35"7	34"7
34"5	57"5	53"	49"2	46"	43"1	40"5	38"3	36"2	35"2
35"	58"3	53"8	50"	46"6	43"7	41"1	38"8	36"8	35"7
35"5	59"1	54"6	50"7	47"3	44"3	41"7	39"4	37"3	36"2
36"	1'00"	55"3	51"4	48"	45"	42"3	40"	37"8	36"7
36"5	1'00"8	56"1	52"1	48"6	45"6	42"9	40"5	38"3	37"2
37"	1'01"6	56"9	52"8	49"3	46"2	43"5	41"1	38"9	37"7

Fig 10   Training intensity tables.

BEST TIME	TRAINING INTENSITY								
	60%	65%	70%	75%	80%	85%	90%	95%	98%
37"5	1'02"5	57"6	53"5	50"	46"8	44"1	41"6	39"4	38"3
38"	1'03"3	58"4	54"2	50"6	47"5	44"7	42"2	39"9	38"8
38"5	1'04"1	59"2	55"	51"3	48"1	45"2	42"7	40"4	39"3
39"	1'05"	59"9	55"7	52"	48"7	45"8	43"3	41"	39"8
39"5	1'05"6	1'00"7	56"4	52"6	49"3	46"4	43"8	41"5	40"3
40"	1'06"6	1'01"5	57"1	53"3	50"	47"	44"4	42"1	40"8
40"5	1'07"5	1'02"2	57"8	54"	50"6	47"6	45"	42"6	41"3
41"	1'08"3	1'03"	58"5	54"6	51"2	48"2	45"5	43"1	41"8
41"5	1'09"1	1'03"8	59"2	55"3	51"8	48"8	46"1	43"6	42"3
42"	1'10"	1'04"5	1'00"	56	52"5	49"4	46"6	44"2	42"8
42"5	1'10"8	1'05"3	1'00"7	56"6	53"1	50"	47"2	44"7	43"4
43"	1'11"6	1'06"1	1'01"4	57"3	53"7	50"5	47"7	45"2	43"9
43"5	1'12"5	1'06"6	1'02"1	58"	54"3	51"1	48"3	45"7	44"4
44"	1'13"3	1'07"6	1'02"8	58"6	55"	51"7	48"8	46"2	44"9
44"5	1'14"1	1'08"4	1'03"5	59"3	55"6	52"3	49"4	46"7	45"4
45"	1'15"	1'09"2	1'04"2	1'00"	56"2	52"9	50"	47"3	45"9
45"5	1'15"8	1'10"	1'05"	1'00"6	56"8	53"5	50"5	47"8	46"4
46"	1'16"6	1'10"7	1'05"7	1'01"3	57"5	54"1	51"1	48"3	46"9
46"5	1'17"5	1'11"5	1'06"4	1'02"	58"1	54"7	51"6	48"8	47"4
47"	1'18"3	1'12"3	1'07"1	1'02"6	58"7	55"2	52"2	49"4	47"9
47"5	1'19"1	1'13"1	1'07"8	1'03"3	59"3	55"8	52"7	50"	48"5
48"	1'20"	1'13"8	1'08"5	1'04"	1'00"	56"4	53"3	50"5	49"
48"5	1'20"6	1'14"6	1'09"2	1'04"6	1'00"6	57"	53"8	51"	49"5
49"	1'21"5	1'15"4	1'10"	1'05"3	1'01"2	57"6	54"4	51"5	50"
49"5	1'22"5	1'16"2	1'10"7	1'06"	1'01"8	58"2	55"	52"	50"5
50"	1'23"3	1'17"	1'11"4	1'06"6	1'02"5	58"8	55"5	52"5	51"
50"5	1'24"1	1'17"7	1'12"1	1'07"3	1'03"1	59"4	56"1	53"	51"5
51"	1'25"	1'18"4	1'12"8	1'08"	1'03"7	1'00"	56"6	53"5	52"
51"5	1'25"8	1'19"2	1'13"5	1'08"6	1'04"3	1'00"5	57"2	54"1	52"2
52"	1'26"6	1'20"	1'14"2	1'09"3	1'05"	1'01"1	57"7	54"7	53"
52"5	1'27"5	1'20"7	1'15"	1'10"	1'05"6	1'01"7	58"3	55"2	53"6
53"	1'28"3	1'21"5	1'15"7	1'10"6	1'06"2	1'02"3	58"8	55"7	54"1
53"5	1'29"1	1'22"3	1'16"4	1'11"3	1'06"8	1'02"9	59"4	56"3	54"6
54"	1'30"	1'23"	1'17"1	1'12"	1'07"5	1'03"5	1'00"	56"8	55"1
54"5	1'30"8	1'23"8	1'17"8	1'12"6	1'08"1	1'04"1	1'00"5	57"3	55"6
55"	1'31"6	1'24"6	1'18"5	1'13"3	1'08"7	1'04"7	1'01"1	57"0	56"1
55"5	1'32"5	1'25"4	1'19"2	1'14"	1'09"3	1'05"2	1'01"6	58"4	56"6
56"	1'33"3	1'26"1	1'20"	1'14"6	1'10"	1'05"8	1'02"2	48"9	57"1
56"5	1'34"1	1'26"9	1'20"7	1'15"3	1'10"5	1'06"4	1'02"7	59"4	57"6
57"	1'35"	1'27"7	1'21"4	1'16"3	1'11"	1'07"	1'03"3	1'00"	58"1
57"5	1'35"6	1'28"5	1'22"1	1'16"6	1'11"8	1'07"6	1'03"8	1'00"5	58"6
58"	1'36"6	1'29"2	1'22"8	1'17"3	1'12"5	1'08"2	1'04"4	1'01"	59"1
58"5	1'37"5	1'30"	1'23"5	1'18"	1'13"1	1'08"8	1'05"	1'01"5	59"6
59"	1'38"3	1'30"7	1'24"2	1'19"6	1'13"7	1'09"4	1'05"5	1'02"1	1'00"2
59"5	1'39"1	1'31"5	1'25"	1'19"3	1'14"3	1'10"	1'06"1	1'02"5	1'00"7
60"	1'40	1'32"3	1'25"7	1'20"	1'15"	1'10"5	1'06"6	1'03"1	1'01"2

1. *Structured fartlek* The route and distance to be run is determined before starting the run as are the fast/slow and hard/easy stages.

2. *Natural fartlek* The route and distance to be run might be decided before the run starts, but the fast/slow and hard/easy stages are not. The runner varies his speed and effort according to how he feels during the run. This requires good self-discipline on the part of the runner if he is to benefit from this type of training.

Heart Rate Monitoring
(*Fig 11*)

The linear relationship between heart rate and oxygen uptake makes the heart rate a convenient indicator of training intensity and recovery. Pulse meters can be worn by the runner during training and are relatively inexpensive. Not only can they give a constant feedback of the pulse during the run, but they can also record heart rates for recall at the end of training. If a pulse meter is not available, the pulse can be recorded using a stop-watch and with reference to *Fig 11*. The pulse can be taken by timing ten beats and then reading the pulse rate off the table. The pulse is found either behind your thumb on the radial (wrist) artery or at the neck on the carotid artery. Use your middle and index fingers to find the pulse and not your thumb as it contains its own pulse. Alternatively, you can place your hand over your chest. The watch is started on a beat; counting starts on the next beat and is stopped on the count of ten.

Time	Rate	Time	Rate
3.0	200	6.6	91
3.1	194	6.7	90
3.2	188	6.8	88
3.3	182	6.9	87
3.4	176	7.0	86
3.5	171	7.1	85
3.6	167	7.2	83
3.7	162	7.3	82
3.8	158	7.4	81
3.9	154	7.5	80
4.0	150	7.6	79
4.1	146	7.7	78
4.2	143	7.8	77
4.3	139	7.9	76
4.4	136	8.0	75
4.5	133	8.1	74
4.6	130	8.2	73
4.7	128	8.3	72
4.8	125	8.4	71
4.9	122	8.5	70.5
5.0	120	8.6	70
5.1	118	8.7	69
5.2	115	8.8	68
5.3	113	8.9	67
5.4	111	9.0	66.5
5.5	109	9.1	66
5.6	107	9.2	65
5.7	105	9.3	64.5
5.8	103	9.4	64
5.9	102	9.5	63
6.0	100	9.6	62.5
6.1	98	9.7	62
6.2	97	9.8	61
6.3	95	9.9	60.5
6.4	94	10.0	60
6.5	92		

Fig 11 Pulse rate table. Take the time of ten beats; against this time read the pulse rate in beats per minute. The watch is started on a beat. Counting starts on the next beat and is stopped on count ten.

3 Speed, Strength and Mobility

When runners with similar levels of aerobic and anaerobic endurance clash, it is often their basic running speed which decides the winner. Speed is an essential attribute for any endurance event and it is as important to develop this aspect of fitness as it is to develop endurance. Running sessions aimed at developing speed are detailed in Chapter 2. These sessions concentrate on the development of stride rate, the ability to move the legs quickly. Running speed, however, is not just related to the rate at which the runner moves but also to the distance covered with each stride.

Speed = Stride Length × Stride Rate

Improvements in stride length will lead to significant improvements in speed. Stride length can be improved through technical training to develop the running action. However, such training can only be successful if the runner has a good range of movement in the joints and adequate levels of strength in the muscle groups involved in the running action.

TECHNICAL TRAINING

The technique used by the endurance runner is a modification of the sprinting action. The faster the run, the closer the technique is to the sprinting action. As relaxation and the conservation of energy are important factors in long runs all unnecessary movement should be limited, so the endurance runner's sprint action has to be more compact than the pure sprinting action, where full range of movement is an advantage.

The Running Action (*Fig 12*)

The action of the runner's legs can be defined as a driving phase and a recovery phase. The driving phase commences when the foot first contacts the ground during a running stride. The bodyweight is supported on the foot, whilst the hips pass over the foot, and the hip, knee and ankle extend to push the runner forwards. The recovery phase starts as the foot leaves the ground. The heel is pulled up towards the buttocks and the thigh is swung through, bringing it parallel to the ground. The lower leg reaches forwards with the foot cocked as the thigh starts to move downwards. Then the lower leg and thigh are swept backwards and downwards in an active pawing action. The foot meets the ground lightly, striking it with the outside edge of the ball of the foot. The foot then rolls towards the inside, bringing the whole of the ball of the foot into contact with the ground.

Even in flat-out sprinting, the trunk remains almost erect with only a slight forwards lean. The arms match the action of the legs, they remain bent and close to

Fig 12   The running action

the body, moving forwards and backwards in a straight line. The arms swing about the shoulders which are kept low. The angle at the elbow changes during the forwards and backwards movements. The hands should be kept relaxed and lightly cupped, with the thumbs resting on the fingers. The head should also be relaxed and carried in natural alignment.

In middle to long distance endurance events, economy of energy is an important consideration. All unnecessary and exaggerated movements should be kept to a minimum. The manner in which the foot strikes the ground changes as the distance being run increases and the speed reduces. The longer the distance, the flatter the foot as it contacts the ground, and in some cases the foot may strike heel first. The trunk has only a slight or no forwards lean, and the arms assist the running action by balancing the rhythm of the legs. The angle at the elbow is less than in sprinting, and there may be a slight crossing of the body. Shoulders remain loose to encourage relaxation.

Running Drills *(Figs 13 to 19)*

The following drills are designed to develop the running action. They involve running over short distances such as 60m at 60–80 per cent effort, but with a sprinting and not a jogging action. During each of these runs, concentration is on one aspect of the running technique only.

1. *Running tall*   The runner concentrates on running tall with high hips and a proud chest.
2. *Low shoulders*   Before starting the run, shrug shoulders to ears, then press them low. Find the feeling of the shoulders being low as you run.
3. *Rear elbow drive*   As you run drive the elbows back and up without allowing the shoulders to rise.
4. *Elbows in*   Keep elbows close to the side as you run and arms swinging backwards and forwards.
5. *Rear leg drive*   Push the ground away and leave the foot in contact with ground a fraction longer.
6. *High knees*   Pick up the knees without sitting back. It is important that you continue to run tall.
7. *Lower leg reach*   Reach out with lower leg and then actively pull your foot back to strike the ground.

Running Drills for Technique

Fig 13   Running tall.

Fig 14   Low shoulders.

Fig 15   Rear elbow drive.

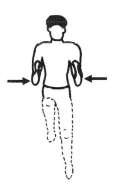

Fig 16   Elbows in.

Fig 17   Rear leg drive.

Fig 18   High knees.

Fig 19   Lower leg reach.

These running drills can either form a specific unit of training themselves, or they can be integrated into the warm-up strides undertaken before serious training. As most runners will include a series of six to eight runs of gradually increasing speed in their warm-up, it is possible to adapt these runs to technique work. This is done by concentrating on a certain aspect of technique during each warm-up sprint.

MOBILITY TRAINING

From our observations of the technique, we can see that running involves the extension and flexion of the ankle, knee, hip and elbow joints, and rotation of the shoulder joints. The degree to which a runner can develop a good technique is determined to some extent by his level of mobility. Mobility is the capacity to perform joint actions through a wide range of movement. Many runners lack mobility in the joints involved in the running action and, as a result, have a short stride length culminating in a poor technique.

Poor mobility prevents runners from learning a good technique and therefore reduces potential for improvement by limiting certain types of conditioning work. Runners lacking mobility have an increased risk of injury and can damage muscles, tendons, ligaments and other connective tissue when attempting to exceed normal ranges of movement. Strains can also be developed from the cumulative stress placed on muscles or connective tissue by compensatory muscular work taking place to accommodate a runner's lack of mobility.

Even in the longer endurance events where ranges of movement are limited, good mobility is essential as it allows free,

Fig 20 *Mobility exercises should be included in every endurance athlete's warm-up routine.*

efficient movement. The runner will be able to develop a good, effective technique which, in turn, will reduce his energy demands. All runners should possess a basic level of all-round mobility and sufficient specific mobility in the hip, knee, ankle and shoulder joints to ensure good technique.

Mobility Exercises
(*Figs 21 to 35*)

It is recommended that suitable mobility exercises for endurance runners (such as those shown) are undertaken as active exercise. Active mobility work involves stretching muscles slowly without any outside assistance, so the runner is always in control. They are called active exercises as the runner has to actively stretch the muscles. When the runner just relaxes and lets a partner stretch the muscles for him he is passive, so this type of mobility work is called passive mobility. The third type of mobility work is the fast swinging and bouncing exercise which inexperienced runners are often seen performing. These exercises, which are called kinetic, can be dangerous if they are attempted before active stretching. The fast bouncing actions can cause muscle damage and instead of warming the runner up may actually cause injury. Passive exercises can also be dangerous unless they are performed with a trained partner. There is always the risk that an untrained partner will force a muscle too far and cause injury. For these reasons, runners are strongly advised to concentrate on active stretching exercises.

Mobility training can be undertaken daily, again as part of the warm-up activities, or, in cases of extremely poor mobility, as a special mobility unit. This depends on whether the runner wishes to develop better mobility or to maintain his present level of mobility.

When performing active mobility exercises the runner should slowly stretch as far as he can, this point is called the end position. Hold the stretch in the end position for 10 seconds, then release the stretch and relax. Repeat the exercise between 10 and 15 times. Whilst performing the exercise, all other parts of the body should be kept as relaxed as possible. It may also help to try and relax the muscles being stretched; concentration on deep breathing helps with this. Raising the body's temperature prior to performing mobility exercises through jogging or striding, or the use of the other gentle warm-up activities, will help increase ranges of movement.

STRENGTH TRAINING

Strength training for endurance runners falls into two broad groups;

1. *General strength* A base of all-round strength and local muscular endurance for the whole body which will allow the runner to accept and benefit from other forms of training and help him to avoid injury.
2. *Special strength* Elastic strength and/or strength endurance which is closely related to the movement pattern and application of force during running.

General strength training, which can take the form of circuit type training using the athlete's bodyweight or a light resistance, has a place in the training of all endurance athletes from the 800m runner to the marathon runner. The importance of other forms of strength training, on the other

Speed, Strength and Mobility

Examples of Suitable Mobility Exercises

Fig 21

Fig 22

Fig 23

Fig 24

Fig 25

Fig 26

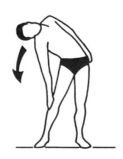

Fig 27

Fig 28

Fig 29

Fig 30

Fig 31

Fig 32

Fig 33

Fig 34

Fig 35

hand, decreases as the duration of the event increases. A larger volume of strength work would be found in the 800m athlete's schedule, than in that of the long distance runner. Such strength training may include routines with barbells, plyometric exercises and resistance runs.

Endurance athletes are interested in developing an improved strength : weight ratio, making them more powerful for their size. They do not wish to increase muscle size and bodyweight as this would decrease their relative VO_2 max. Their training is therefore aimed at developing improved neuro-muscular co-ordination and anaerobic enzyme activity, which is best achieved through elastic strength and strength endurance training.

Two schools of thought exist on how strength is best developed, one that the muscle groups involved in the running action should be trained through conventional exercises, and the other that strength training must replicate the running action. Both approaches produce results but scientific evidence strongly supports the latter, so, whilst both approaches are advocated, it is essential that exercises which resemble the running action be included in training programmes.

Strength training can take the form of:

1. Circuit training   *General training*
2. Weight training   *Special training*
3. Resistance runs   *Special training*
4. Plyometric exercises   *Special training*

Circuit Training (*Figs 36 & 37*)

Circuit training is used to develop general all-round strength and local muscular endurance. A basic circuit should include exercises aimed at developing the arms, shoulders, trunk and legs. Fitness is developed by gradually building up the numbers of sets and repetitions to be completed in each session. As the runner develops, he can make the circuit more demanding by adding resistance or by altering each exercise to make it more difficult. Circuits can also be designed which will make use of the fixed weight machines.

Circuit training can be made more stressful by arranging the exercises in a form known as stage training. In circuit training, when one set of an exercise is completed, the athlete moves on to the next exercise, and so on until each of the exercises has been completed once. The circuit is then repeated until all sets have been completed. In stage training, the athlete completes one set of an exercise, has a short break, then repeats a second set, and so on until all the sets of that exercise have been completed. Then the athlete moves on to the next exercise. Another possibility is to group two exercises together, one exercise acting as the recovery period for the other.

Dips

Sit-ups

Burpees

Step-ups

Back raise

Press-ups

Fig 36   A basic circuit.

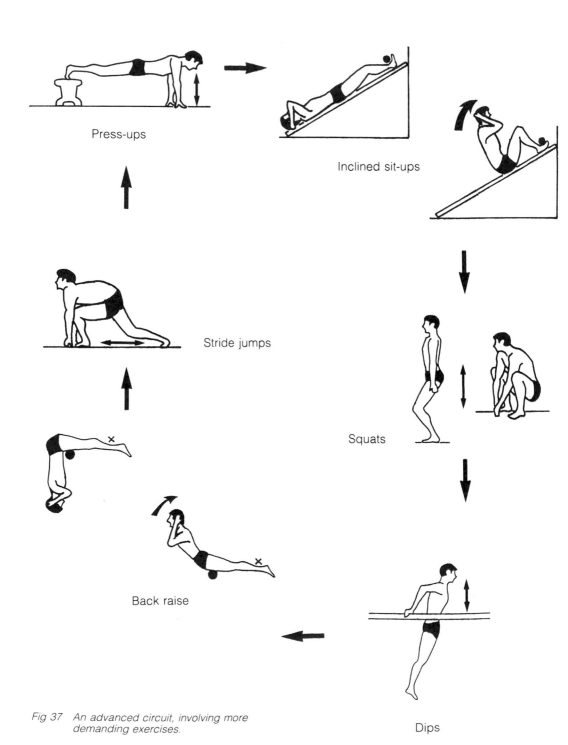

Press-ups

Inclined sit-ups

Stride jumps

Squats

Back raise

Dips

Fig 37   An advanced circuit, involving more
demanding exercises.

Weight Training (*Figs 38 to 41*)

Endurance athletes using weight training have traditionally lifted light weights using high repetitions of 15 to 20, or even higher in certain cases. This type of activity develops strength endurance and is similar in nature to circuit training. Recently, middle-distance runners have started to lift weights of 75–90 per cent maximum with repetitions of about 4 to 6. This type of training develops strength but does not lead to unnecessary muscle bulk. Elastic strength is an important quality for the middle-distance runner and can be developed through this type of weight training.

Fig 38   Back squat.

Fig 39   Bench press.

Fig 40   Press behind neck.

Fig 41   Cleans.

Resistance Runs (*Figs 42 to 44*)

Repeated runs against added resistance form exercises which closely resemble the specific movement pattern of running itself. The resistance can take the form of a hill, a weight carried on the body, a drag which has to be pulled, or sprinting over sand (although sand does tend to give way).

Another activity which can be grouped with resistance runs is sprint drills, such as the high knee drill when performed over long distances. These drills are normally performed over short distances to develop running technique and leg speed, but when performed over extended distances they become a strength endurance activity.

Fig 42   Hill runs.

Fig 43   Towing.

Plyometrics (*Figs 45 to 48*)

The term plyometrics refers to elastic strength exercises such as hopping, bounding and depth jumps. These exercises replicate the muscle dynamics of the running action, and exercises such as bounding are also close to the running action. Performed over distances ranging from 30m to 100m they make the muscles of the legs work actively and elastically during each foot contact.

Fig 44   Weighted jacket.

Fig 45   High knee hops

Fig 46   Bounding.

Fig 47   Squat jumps

Fig 48   Skipping for height.

4 Endurance Training Programmes

ANNUAL TRAINING PROGRAMMES
(*Figs 49 & 50*)

The training methods outlined in Chapters 2 and 3 need to be organised into a training programme for the runner. The amounts of each type of training to be included in the programme will vary from runner to runner, depending on their event, individual strengths and weaknesses, stage of development and the time of year. Most runners organise their training on a weekly basis, changing the emphasis of the training each month. A long term plan, usually a year, is established in order to give the training programme a sense of direction, training being geared for a specific set of competitions.

The annual training programme is divided up into four distinct periods:

1. *Transition period*   A period of recuperation, during which the runner recovers from the fatigue of the previous competition period.
2. *General preparation period*   A period of foundation training during which general aerobic fitness, mobility, general strength and local muscular endurance are developed. This is a period of training to develop fitness which will allow the runner to accept and benefit from specific forms of training.
3. *Special training period*   A period containing training to develop the specific fitness required to meet the demands of the runner's event.
4. *Competition period*   A period of competition in which training is aimed at preparing the runner for important competition.

Month	Nov	Dec	Jan	Feb	Mar	Apr	May	Jun	Jul	Aug	Sep	Oct
Phase	General				Special			Competition				Tran
Period	Preparation							Competition				Tran

Fig 49   *An annual training programme for a middle-distance runner who specialises on the track and does not prepare specifically for an indoor or cross-country period (although he may undertake a few of these events).*

Month	Nov	Dec	Jan	Feb	Mar	Apr	May	Jun	Jul	Aug	Sep	Oct
Phase	General		Spec	Indoors		General		Spec	Track Comp			Tran
Period	Preparation			Comp		Preparation			Comp			Tran

Fig 50   An annual training plan featuring two competitive periods. The year is broken into two training cycles with a winter competition period (indoors or cross-country) and a summer competition period (track). This runner prepares specifically for both the winter and summer competitions.

Training Principles

When laying down annual training programmes and planning the content of the weekly and monthly schedules, a number of training principles need to be considered.

Overload

The work-load has to be sufficiently demanding to encourage the body to adapt and improve performance capacity. The volume and intensity of all forms of training can be determined with this in mind.

Progression

The work-load must gradually increase as the runner adapts to previous loadings. The volume of aerobic training (mileage/km) will steadily increase over the general preparation period and the quality (speed) of aerobic and anaerobic work will gradually improve over the special preparation period. Training loads often progress every four weeks. Most runners would complete three weeks of hard training followed by a fourth easy or recovery week. The training load would then be advanced for the next four week cycle.

Specificity

The effects of training are specific to the individual runner and to the type of work being undertaken. Training needs to be set for the individual if he is to gain maximum benefit. The training load should be related to the runner's present level of fitness and to his competitive event.

Reversibility

The improvements in performance capacity gained as a result of training reverse once training stops. The rate at which they are lost will be similar to the rate at which they were gained. Runners with years of aerobic running behind them will lose fitness more slowly than those who have only taken up the sport recently.

Recovery

Recovery is an important part of the training load. It is during the recovery period after training is complete that adaptation takes place. Many runners ignore this fact and allow insufficient recovery in their training schedules. As a result they do not progress at the rate they would like and many suffer from overtraining symptoms. As a rule there should be 48 to 72 hours between similar types of anaerobic training. Aerobic training runs, on the other hand, do not place the runner under great stress and so more than one run can be completed on the same day.

Goal Setting

The training programme will prepare the runner for selected competitions. It is these competitions which give the programme its direction. Care should be taken when selecting competitions, as it is important that the goals set should, on the one hand, be realistically attainable and, on the other, be sufficiently demanding to encourage the runner to strive for success. These goals do not necessarily need to involve the winning of a race, they can be goals such as bettering personal best performances and placings.

Middle-distance Programme

The following outline programme gives an example of how the training year is divided and the types of training which are included for a middle-distance runner.

Transitional Period

The runner will undertake low intensity aerobic runs of a medium duration but keep his total weekly mileage low. Mobility work and other forms of exercise, such as swimming, games, etc., will be included in the schedule. Training is kept informal and low key.

General Preparation Period

If the runner is preparing for a track season and is using an annual training programme similar to that illustrated in *Fig 50*, this period could last as long as six or seven months. There will be a gradual increase in the weekly training mileage, which should level out towards the end of the period. Whilst training will comprise a mixture of aerobic and anaerobic forms, the main emphasis will be on the development of aerobic endurance.

A typical programme would include:

1 × long duration run (example: 12 miles)
1 × fast medium duration run (example: 3–4 miles)
5 or more × steady medium duration runs (example: 4–7 miles)
1 × extensive interval run (example: 4 or 5 4-min runs)
1 × long or short hill run
1–2 × circuit training/weight training
Mobility training
Speed/skill training
Occasional cross-country or road races

Special Preparation Period

This period will usually be half the duration of the general preparation period. The emphasis in training shifts towards the specific demands of the runner's event. Total mileage is reduced but the quality of training is improved. There is a shift from aerobic to anaerobic training methods without neglecting the maintenance of aerobic endurance levels.

A typical programme would include:

1 × long duration run (example as before)
1 × short hill session
5 or more × steady medium duration runs (example as before)
2 × short repetition/short recovery anaerobic intervals
(example: 3 × [4 × 300m])

2 × long repetition/long duration runs
(example: 4 × 1,000m)
Speed work
Specific strength training (example: bounding)

Competition Period

The training during this period will be aimed at maintaining both general and specific conditioning and at preparing the runner for competition. The actual content of training will be dictated by the dates of competitions, the runner reducing the training load as competition approaches.

Marathon Programme

The following programme would be set over a period of six months and would be aimed at preparing the marathon runner for a specific race.

Transitional Period

The transitional period would last one month and would be a period of recovery from the last marathon. The reduced training programme would mainly feature slow to steady paced medium duration runs. Other activities, such as swimming, cycling, any sports, mobility and circuit training, might be undertaken during this period. The emphasis is on full recovery from the last marathon.

General Preparation Period

This period will last about three months and, as with the middle-distance runner's programme, will feature a gradual increase in the total weekly mileage. The mileage will be higher than that achieved by the middle-distance runner, as there is a greater emphasis in the marathon runner's programme on steady paced medium, and steady and slow paced long duration running. The weekly programme will also feature at least one training session aimed at improving the runner's aerobic power, i.e. an extensive aerobic interval, a fartlek, or a short fast continuous run. Alternatively, a Gerschler type interval training session will help develop running technique, speed or pace. Some time should also be found for mobility training and for circuit training or hillwork to develop general strength and local muscular endurance.

Special Preparation Period

The base of steady paced medium duration runs and slow and steady paced long duration runs is continued during this phase. In addition to the one session per week of training to develop aerobic power, some road races are introduced. Long duration runs at marathon pace are introduced and a slow long duration run of two to three hours is included, normally one of these runs being attempted every two to three weeks. Some general training for speed, strength and mobility is also maintained. The total weekly mileage is not necessarily increased during this phase but is maintained, allowing the quality to improve.

Competition Period

This period is fairly short as it comprises the 'taper' (gradual reduction of training load) for the marathon race. A two week taper may be chosen during which the runner will reduce his training load, in order to arrive at the starting line for the marathon fresh and hungry to do well. The content of this period will vary according to the runner.

5 Competition, Clothing and Climate

COMPETITION

There are many competitive opportunities for the endurance runner over varying distances and underfoot conditions. Events range from the standard Olympic track events, road races and cross-country running to related events such as fell-running and ultra-distance races.

The current Olympic track and road events are:

Middle distance	800m	Men & women
	1,500m	Men & women
Long distance	3,000m	Women
	5,000m	Men
	10,000m	Men & women
Steeplechase	3,000m	Men
Marathon	Marathon	Men & women

Cross-country races are run over a set range of distances, with approximate distances for the world championships. The following are the IAAF cross-country distances:

Group	Competition Distances	World Championships
Men	7–14km	12km (approx)
Women	5–10km	8km (approx)
Junior men	2–5km	4km (approx)

With the exception of the 3,000m steeple-chase, all the endurance events are flat races. In the steeplechase, runners have to negotiate three-foot (91.4cm) high wooden hurdles and a water jump. To be effective in this event the skills of hurdling and water jumping need to be perfected. Once the two techniques have been mastered, hurdles can be used in track interval sessions to develop the runner's ability to pick-out the hurdles whilst fatigued and to run over them without disrupting pace.

Steeplechasing

The steeplechase is one of the most rewarding of the endurance track events and should certainly be introduced to young endurance runners as early as possible. Many runners miss the chance of being successful in this event by neglecting to learn the skills of hurdling and water jump clearance when they are young. Steeplechasing not only demands a middle-distance runner's endurance background, but also requires the ability to clear the barriers with as little variation in running pace as possible. To do this, the steeplechaser develops a hurdling technique which allows him to negotiate the hurdle without overtaxing his energy resources.

Hurdling Technique (Fig 51)

Steeplechasers, like sprint hurdlers, require good levels of mobility – in particular, good hip mobility. Good hurdling technique is only possible when the runner has a good level of hip mobility. Exercises which specifically develop this are shown

Fig 51   Steeplechase barrier clearance.

in *Figs 21 to 35.*

Hurdling is best introduced to a runner using ordinary hurdles, rather than steeplechase barriers. These hurdles can be lowered, allowing the endurance runner to learn the hurdling technique gradually. The runner should be asked to run over the top of the hurdles and be discouraged from jumping them. Placing hurdles a set distance apart, the runner is encouraged to take three, five or seven strides between them; this allows each hurdle to be taken with the same lead leg. Hurdles can also be set to accommodate four, six or eight strides, in order to develop the use of alternate lead legs. Once a runner has established a set rhythm between hurdles, the barriers should be gradually increased in height until they reach three feet (91.4cm), the height of a steeplechase barrier.

The following points of hurdling technique should be taught:

1.   The runner should lean into the hurdle prior to running over it.
2.   The runner should pick up his lead leg bent and high.
3.   The lead leg should be picked up and placed down in a straight line.
4.   The heel of the trail foot should be tucked in towards the bottom and the knee should be brought up towards the armpit. It should then be brought across the hurdle and round the front of the body into the sprinting position.
5.   The opposite arm to the lead leg should balance the runner by reaching across the hurdle, whilst the other arm is held at the side. As the runner comes off the hurdle both arms are brought round into the sprinting position.

Water Jump Technique (Fig 52)

In the water jump technique, the runner places his foot on top of the barrier and drives out across the water. This is best taught using a low barrier and gradually increasing its height to three feet. A barrier placed over a long jump sand-pit can be used instead of the actual water jump.

The first requirement of the runner is to step on and off the barrier without loss of rhythm. The runner is then asked to perform this activity but to leave his foot on the hurdle longer, which will help to develop the split off the top of the jump. Any forward rotation can be countered by driving up the trailing knee. The key points to watch at this stage are:

47

Start

Finish

Fig 52   The water jump clearance technique.

1.   Get close enough to the barrier to allow a good drive on to the hurdle. Lean into the barrier, drive up and forwards with a good knee.

2.   Place your foot firmly on top of the hurdle.

3.   Keep your centre of gravity low over the barrier and keep the forwards speed going.

4.   Achieve a good split or drive over the water by keeping your foot in contact with the barrier for as long as possible to ensure a good leg extension.

5.   Keep your free knee high as you drive off the hurdle to avoid forwards rotation.

Tactics

When runners line up at the start of a race, they aim either to win or to achieve a best performance in terms of their time or placing in the race. Not every runner expects to have a chance of winning a race, so they sensibly set themselves other performance targets. Each runner has to decide how best to run the race in order to achieve his target. This is not always an easy decision to make as a number of different factors can influence the outcome of a race, including weather conditions and other runners' racing tactics.

For the runner who is not concerned with winning but aims to run the fastest possible time, the best plan is to run as close as possible to even pace. In a good quality field this can prove difficult, as the better runners tend to set a fast early pace. Novice runners who lack experience of pace often get caught up in the fast early pace and suffer the consequences in the

Fig 53   Irish international Marcus O'Sullivan moves strongly to the front of
the field to cover the leaders Steve Ovett (7) and Tim Hutchings (3).

closing stages of the race. Few races are won as a result of even paced running, so the runner who hopes to become a winner must be capable of responding to different racing tactics.

Middle-distance Events

With the middle-distance events, 800m and 1,500m, the racing pace is fast, leaving no room for error. There is a need to maintain contact with the leaders and to cover all moves by running close to the front of the pack. Running at the back of the field is unwise unless the runner knows that he is very much better than the rest of the opposition. It is best to run in the leading group, usually on the shoulder of the leading runner – a position which allows the runner to cover all breaks. From this position the runner will be able to take the lead and attempt to outrun his opponents to the line.

In deciding when to go for the finishing tape, the runner will need to know his own strengths and weaknesses in terms of speed endurance and hopefully those of his opposition. He needs to know whether he could outsprint his opponents in the last 100m of the race or whether he needs to go for the finishing tape much earlier. If he knows that several of the other runners have better sprint finishes than him, he may decide to make the running hard over the last 300m or more. By doing this, he will hope to sap the finishing sprint out of the opposition. Some middle-distance runners try to do this by setting a fast pace from the front throughout the race.

In the 800m, the first 100m is run in lanes, after which the runners break for the inside lane. In the 1,500m, the runners break from the start of the race. All runners need to remain alert from the start to avoid being knocked over or boxed in to a position from which it is difficult to cover all moves during the race. Some runners will get caught behind others and will not have enough space through which to accelerate either to cover moves or to break away from the field. A fair amount of physical contact occurs between runners in middle-distance races as they jostle with each other in an attempt to stay in the best possible position. Middle-distance runners should stamp their authority on each race, responding to moves or making an attempt to break the field with strength and conviction.

Longer Distances

The track races of 3,000m, 5,000m and 10,000m take longer to complete and allow alternative strategies to be employed during the race. One tactic is to dominate the race from start to finish by leading with a fast sustained pace. Another is to run behind the leading runners, waiting to inject a fast finishing pace over later stages of the race. A third possibility is to alternate fast and slow laps in an effort to disrupt the oppositions' rhythm and to sap the strength of the fast finishers. A good general rule for all runners to remember is that when they pass another runner they should do so with conviction.

On the roads or in cross-country, tactics are similar to those used by the longer distance track runners. One difference is that the terrain being covered is variable, so runners can decide to increase their pace whilst the pack is negotiating a demanding stage of the course, for example whilst running up a steep gradient.

*Fig 54   Cross-country running – a popular form of competition for
endurance runners during the winter months.*

CLOTHING AND FOOTWEAR

As the popularity of endurance running competition grew in the early 1980s, the number of manufacturers and retailers of athletic footwear for runners expanded. Today there is a wide range of clothing and footwear available to the runner, both fashionable and practical, through the many sports shops who specialise in running equipment.

Running Shoes

The most important item of equipment required by the runner is the pair of shoes on his feet. Special running shoes are available for both training and racing on road, cross-country and track. There is a wide choice of different styles of shoe, each with its individual characteristics. It is essential that the right type of shoe is selected by the runner which will suit his shape of foot, mileage and running mechanics.

Training Shoes

Most running is completed in training shoes and it is not uncommon for runners to wear out several pairs in a year. It is important that they are comfortable to wear and that they provide the runner with protection against injury. They must be selected carefully to ensure that they fit well and that they are suitable for the runner's structure and running style.

Training shoes are best purchased at a specialist running shop, where the assistants have some knowledge of running and can advise on the qualities of the different models they stock. Late afternoon is the best time to try on shoes, as your feet swell slightly as the day progresses. It is also wise to wear a pair of socks of the type used during training. They should be snug fitting but not too tight. Look for a good half an inch between the big toe and the toe box.

Each of the different models of training shoe will have been designed to suit the needs of a particular type of runner's foot structure and running style. Most training shoes incorporate features to cope with stress caused by forces which occur when the foot strikes the ground and by the excessive sideways movement of the foot whilst still in contact with the ground. Materials such as ethylene vinyl acetate (EVA), which absorb shock, and features such as external heel counters, which control excessive sideways movement, are incorporated into the design of training shoes to take account of these problems.

During running, some people strike the ground initially with their heels and then roll up on the ball of the foot to push off. Others land flat-footed and some strike the ground with the ball or front of the foot. In general, the faster the athlete runs, the more he tends to strike the ground with the front part of the foot. In addition to the action of the foot rolling from the heel towards the toes, it also contacts the ground with the outside edge and rolls over to the inside edge to push off. This inward rotation is called *pronation* and most athletes do this, some to such an extent that they are said to be over-pronating. There are a few runners, *supinators,* who do the opposite and roll from the inside edge to the outside edge.

As most runners pronate, most training shoes are designed to combat excessive pronation. Unfortunately, these shoes do not suit those athletes who supinate and, in fact, are likely to cause them injury by increasing the outward rotation. Care needs to be taken to ensure that the wrong type of shoe is not selected.

Parts of a Training Shoe (Fig 55)

(a) *Arch support* Extra material inside the shoe which supports the arches.
(b) *External heel counter support* A nylon collar supporting the heel counter and helping to prevent excessive sideways movement of the foot inside the shoe.
(c) *Heel counter* Rigid cup of material which wraps around the heel to hold it in place.
(d) *Heel tab* Tab which protrudes from the top of the heel counter which, if hard, can sometimes aggravate the Achilles tendon. A low tab is preferable.
(e) *Insock* Insert usually made of EVA covered with knitted material which goes into the shoe and fills the gap between the foot and the shoe.
(f) *Midsole* Shock absorbing layer between uppers and outsole.

(g) *Outsole* The part of the shoe that comes into contact with the ground.

Spikes

Care has to be taken when selecting spikes to ensure they have been designed for use by endurance runners and not sprinters. Sprinters tend to run on the ball of the foot, so their spiked shoes offer little protection for the heel. The longer the distance the more likely it is that the runner's weight will fall back on to his heels, and it is important, therefore, that the spikes afford heel protection. The spikes for sprinters have rounded heels, those for endurance runners have a heel wedge.

Running Wear

In competition, the runner requires a pair of shorts and a running vest, usually in his club colours. Vests should not be tight-fitting and should have plenty of room under the arm. They can be made of a

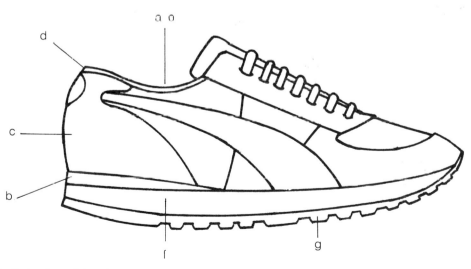

Fig 55 Parts of a training shoe.

mesh material or a combination of mesh and nylon. Nylon is more usual as it is light and easy to launder, although some runners still prefer cotton vests.

Freedom shorts, which are briefly cut but airy and loose-fitting around the legs and crotch, are popular with both male and female runners. They are secure at the waist and should have an inner, which does away with the need for underwear. Some female runners have a preference for the more traditional briefs-type of shorts.

Socks should be worn with training and competition shoes to cut down the possibil-ity of blisters and to provide some cushion-ing. Female runners can purchase a spe-cial sports bra, which is available from several manufacturers.

For warming-up or training purposes the runner will need other warm clothing. This could include long or short-sleeved T-shirts, training tights, track suit, tracksters, sweat-top, and a wet weather suit or shower top. In very cold weather, gloves and hats are also worn. The runner will need a stock of training and competition clothing, as he will need to launder clothing daily.

Fig 56 Betty Van Steenbroek (Belgium), Susan Tooby (Wales), Roisin Smyth (Ireland) and Yvonne Murray (Scotland) display a range of warm clothing that was certainly needed to cope with the cold and wet conditions at an international cross-country event.

THE RUNNING ENVIRONMENT

At sea-level and in temperate climatic conditions the runner has few problems with his environment. Training at altitude offers some advantage to the endurance runner on his return to sea-level, whilst competing in hot conditions can cause problems for endurance performance. The endurance runner needs to have an understanding of both altitude and heat.

Altitude

Runners who usually live, train and compete at around sea-level will experience difficulty exercising at altitude, due to the lower ambient atmospheric pressures. Less oxygen is available to the runner for aerobic activity, as the reduced pressure of oxygen in the lungs means that less oxygen can be taken up by haemoglobin. When runners train at altitude, adaptation takes place in response to the shortage of oxygen. This involves an increase in haemoglobin levels and in the oxygen carrying capacity of the blood. It may also involve an increase in the levels of myoglobin in the working muscles. This super-compensation effect gives the runner a distinct advantage when he returns to sea-level; an advantage which is possessed by athletes who live at altitude and race at sea-level.

Altitude training is undertaken by many successful international performers, and there are some who spend most of their preparation period at altitude. Training periods last a minimum of three weeks at heights of 5,000 to 10,000 feet (1,500 to 3,000m). On return to sea-level it will take about six weeks for adaptations to revert to normal values. At these heights VO_2max will fall by about 15 to 20 per cent but will slowly adapt at about one per cent per week at altitude. Although VO_2max will not rise to pre-altitude values, there will be a marked improvement when the runner first returns to sea-level.

Training in the first week at altitude should be of a low intensity, with high intensity training starting in the second week after acute adaptations to altitude have occurred.

Heat

Runners need to guard against the potential problems which occur with training and competing in hot environments, such as dehydration, heat exhaustion, sun-stroke and heat-stroke. Body temperature rises with exercise as a result of increased energy production. The heat produced by energy production has to be constantly removed if the body is not to overheat. In hot environments it is harder for the runner to dissipate heat and so he is at risk to heat-related problems.

Increases in body temperature lead to an increase in blood flow out towards the body surface. This excess surface heat is then lost through convection (air passing over skin), radiation (heat taken up by cooler air), conduction (heat taken up by cooler objects), the air breathed out and evaporation of sweat.

If the air temperature is low, heat will be lost by the body. However, in hot environments the temperature of the air is high which does not help heat loss; and if the air temperature is higher than 33–34°C (92°F), heat will be absorbed not lost. The body will also absorb the heat radiating from the sun and this will add to the problem of losing the heat generated by exercise. Running in a light-coloured singlet will help the runner to avoid absorbing too much heat by reflecting the sun's rays. The air will cool the runner as it passes over his body surface whilst running, and the wind will provide a further cooling effect.

Heat is also lost in the water vapour that is breathed out. In a cold environment a mist of water vapour can be seen as you breathe out and it is not uncommon on a cold night to heat up your hands by blowing on them. When it is hot, however, very little heat is lost in this way.

Most body heat in hot environments is lost through the evaporation of sweat from the body surface, and this is easiest in a hot dry climate. Sweating leads to loss of body fluid which, if excessive, will lead to a fall in running efficiency. A 2 per cent weight loss can lead to a 20 per cent drop in the muscles' working capacity. Dehydration can be a major problem in endurance running in hot climates. In hot humid climates the air is heavily saturated with moisture and the evaporation of sweat is inhibited. The runner continues to sweat, losing fluid and risking dehydration, but becomes ineffective in losing heat. Overheating and dehydration can lead to *heat exhaustion.*

Heat Exhaustion

The symptoms of heat exhaustion are a normal body temperature, cold sweaty skin, drowsiness, weakness, vomiting, an elevated pulse and hypertension. It can be prevented by regularly drinking water prior to and during the race or training session.

Prior to a race, the runner should sip water often in the three hour period between his last meal and the start of the race. In the 30 minutes immediately before the race the runner should drink half a pint

of water and he should then drink every 20 to 25 minutes during the race. It is also important to drink frequently after the race to replace fluid.

The runner who is forced to stop with heat exhaustion should rest in a cool, airy place and should try to sip water in order to rehydrate.

Sunstroke

If the head or back of the neck is exposed to the direct rays of the sun during an endurance run, the runner risks developing sunstroke. Sunstroke is not related to heat loss but results from the effect of heat on the brain. It can be prevented by not running during the hottest part of the day and by wearing a hat which provides cover for the head and the back of the neck. The hat can be soaked with water prior to running.

Symptoms include red skin, swollen face, buzzing in the ears, dizziness, headache, nausea, sleepiness, elevated pulse, weakness and rapid respiration. The runner will probably be unable to continue and may collapse. If despite the sunstroke he manages to continue running, he may develop *heat-stroke.*

Runners with sunstroke should stop all activity, be removed to a cool, well-ventilated area, their clothes should be removed and an ice bag or cold compress should be applied to the forehead and the back of the neck.

Heat-stroke

Heat-stroke is the end result of overheating and marks a total breakdown in heat regulation. This rare condition is marked by a high temperature, hot, dry red skin, and signs of confusion, loss of control, or even collapse. The treatment is to remove the runner to a cool, airy place, undress him and wrap him in a blanket soaked in cold water. Ensure that he has plenty of ventilation. If spectators gather round to observe the casualty, clear them away. It may be necessary to immerse the runner in a bath of cold water to bring the temperature down. If the runner is still conscious he should be asked to sip water. Medical attention will be necessary in a case of heat-stroke.

It is much better to be well prepared and to prevent cases of heat exhaustion by being careful to take the following steps:

1. Avoid running during the hottest part of the day, run when it is cooler.
2. Remember that it takes time to acclimatise to heat; until this occurs reduce the intensity and extent of endurance running.
3. Avoid wearing too much clothing, wear loose clothes which allow the air to circulate and light coloured clothing that reflects the sun's rays.
4. Wear white or light-coloured head gear that gives protection to the head and to the neck.
5. Drink sufficient fluids, before, during and after training and competition. Sprinkle water over yourself during runs, especially over head, neck and thighs. Use showers in races.
6. Get used to sweating.
7. Never run immediately after a meal as the blood is drawn towards the gut and is not as effective at transferring heat to the body surface.
8. Reduce the amount of running during warm-up in hot weather.
9. Warm-down immediately after training or competing, as passive rest will lead to the runner cooling down too quickly.
10. Never enter a shower or sauna immediately after running; always give yourself time to warm-down first.

6 The Young Endurance Runner

Many children and adolescents take part in endurance running and are involved in regular training. It is hoped that their participation in the sport as young people will be continued into their adult lives. This, unfortunately, does not happen in a large number of cases. Many children achieve success as a result of undertaking heavy training programmes and find themselves unable to progress at a later stage of their development. Some drop out of the sport because they are no longer enjoying the activity. Others suffer injury caused by training loads which are not appropriate to their stage of physical development and as a result are unable to continue in the sport.

PHYSICAL DEVELOPMENT

Stages of Development
(*Fig 57*)

As children and adolescents are still developing physically, psychologically and socially, it is important that the stages of development which link childhood and adulthood are understood. This knowledge will allow training programmes which are appropriate to the growing athlete to be set, instead of trying to fit young people to training programmes designed for adults.

The stages of development for males and females are shown in *Fig 57*. These are shown against an estimated time-scale; it is not possible to be more specific since each individual matures at a different rate. It is possible for one girl to reach menarche at twelve years, whilst another girl may not reach this stage until she is eighteen. As a rule, most girls mature earlier than boys, but it is equally true that not all girls mature before all boys. The stages of development are shown together with some of the significant physiological changes that occur.

Physiological Changes

Prior to the pre-pubertal growth spurt, around eight to nine years of age, a young person's mobility starts to decline. So even at this young age there is a need to introduce mobility training.

Before puberty males and females have similar maximal oxygen uptakes. At puberty this starts to decline steadily in girls around ten years of age, until maturity is reached at around sixteen to seventeen years of age. Absolute maximal aerobic power does increase over this period, but changes to body composition and the cardio-vascular system have a negative influence on relative values. With boys, relative maximal oxygen uptake continues to increase from puberty through to maturity at twenty-one years of age. Thus, relative VO_2max declines in girls following puberty, whilst it continues to develop in boys.

Anaerobic power, both alactic and lactic, matures about the same time as aerobic

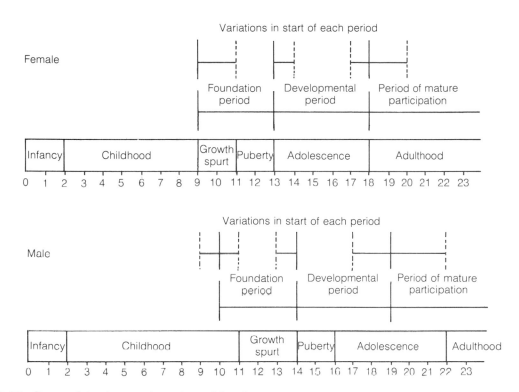

Fig 57   Stages of development for males and females.

power. Around puberty, there is a rapid rise of the female oestrogen hormones in girls and of the male androgen hormones in boys. The female hormones discourage muscular development whilst male hormones encourage it.

The skeleton matures in girls around eighteen years of age and in boys about twenty-two years. Prior to this the bones, in particular the growing ends of the long bones and the bones of the spine, are easily damaged.

Periods of Development

The nature and rates of different physiological, psychological and social changes lead us to recommend that young people should pass through two distinct periods of preparation, before eventually participating in endurance events as mature adults: the foundation period which commences at around nine to eleven years, and the developmental period which commences at around thirteen years.

The Foundation Period

The foundation period lasts between three to four years with the emphasis on fun and enjoyment through involvement in games and fun activities. General training in the form of simple mobility exercises, body-weight strength exercises and aerobic endurance activity is undertaken, together with training to develop speed and skill. It is important to develop basic skills and rhythm during this period. Training one day

Fig 58 *As a rule, girls mature earlier than boys.*

per week is gradually increased to three days per week, with variety of activity being important.

The Developmental Period

The developmental period lasts between four to six years. In the first years the emphasis is on general training, allowing the athlete to develop an all-round base of mobility, aerobic endurance, local muscular endurance and strength, with the aim of enabling him to accept and benefit from specific training.

Over the last two years the percentage of specific work gradually increases. During this period appropriate training and competition behaviour is established. Athletes learn to train in a disciplined manner, on a regular basis and to compete with good sportsmanship. During these last two years the barbell techniques of weight training are learned, using loadings at 60 per cent of the estimated single maximum repetition. Training three days per week at the beginning of this period increases to six per week during the final two years.

Mature Participation

Between the ages of seventeen and twenty-two the period of mature participation commences, and it is important that this period should not commence earlier or later than these ages. As the runner becomes more experienced, the percentage of specific training increases – the time spent in training depending on the commitment of the runner. With elite runners this will be daily, with training probably taking place on more than one occasion each day.

TRAINING

Endurance Training

Children and adolescents should be encouraged to take part in aerobic endurance activity, although loadings will be easier than those undertaken by adults in terms of both the intensity and the volume. Aerobic endurance can be trained and improved at any stage of development, but the notion that the cardio-vascular system can be enhanced by training before, during or after puberty has not been substantiated. With young people, the volume of training should be kept low and the quality of training emphasised.

Anaerobic training is best introduced after puberty and, as with aerobic training, the volume is relatively low and the quality

high. Sufficient recovery to enable the young athlete to maintain the quality during training is important.

Short term duration training, both for aerobic and anaerobic endurance, should be used initially with the young runner. Volumes of training can then be gradually increased to include at first medium and then long term duration training.

Variety is an important factor in the young athlete's training programme, reducing the possibility of over-use injury and helping to keep the young person motivated. Competition for young people should involve events of different distances on track, road and country. Training sessions should be made enjoyable by keeping them novel. The following are ideas:

1. *Whistle fartlek* Coach uses whistle to indicate pre-planned pace.
2. *Indian file fartlek* The squad run spaced 5–10m apart, and the last man sprints to front of file. Variations include weaving in and out of the squad of runners or two runners together on either side of file.
3. *Terrain fartlek* Coach puts squad out over a pre-set course with set cues such as run hard uphill, sprint on flat sections, jog down hill, etc.
4. *Fox and hounds fartlek* A fox or various foxes are given a lead in a restricted area and the other athletes must catch them.
5. *Continuous relays* Using a 400m track or circuit and team of 5 runners. Runners 1 and 5 stand at the start/finish, 2 at 100m, 3 at 200m, 4 at 300m. Run for a set time or for a set number of laps.
6. *Paarlauf* A continuous relay with 2 runners. On a 400m track the first runner runs 200m and passes baton to second runner who also runs 200m. Whilst runner is completing the 200m stretch, the partner

*Fig 59 Endurance competition for young athletes should involve cross-
          country running.*

jogs across the track back to his starting point to receive the baton.

7. *Timed team runs* Decide on a set time, say 30 seconds, place flags from 150m to 200m at 10m intervals. Blow a whistle for start and finish of 30 second period. Athletes run for 30 seconds and are awarded points for their team according to which flag they reach.

Mobility Training

Mobility training should commence with children as young as nine years of age and should be continued throughout the runner's life. A variety of exercise, involving all of the body's joint actions, is important to develop all-round mobility, rather than specific mobility for running (some suitable exercises are shown in *Figs 21 to 35*). Exercises which feature the runner actively contracting muscles are preferred to passive or kinetic exercises, as the young person has control over the stretching action. These active exercises are safer than passive and kinetic work which require greater care and constant supervision.

Strength Training

Simple forms of strength training can be introduced to the young runner around nine or ten years of age. This training should take the form of partner games, climbing activities, hopping relays, games with benches, boxes, medicine balls, and so on. Torso exercises which strengthen the musculature supporting the spine, such as sit-ups, back raises and lateral bends, should be included. One unit of strength training a week will suffice, and it should include a large variety of exercises.

At thirteen or fourteen years of age, training for strength becomes slightly more formal. Circuit training, with its progression of repetitions and sets, is introduced. Exercises need to be carefully selected to ensure that all major muscle groups are being worked. Simple exercises should be chosen and they need to be well taught, ensuring a full range of movement. The sets, repetitions and recovery periods should be calculated to allow athletes to maintain the quality of movement in each exercise.

Weight training can be introduced around sixteen to seventeen years of age, possibly using the multi-gym as a starting point, and keeping repetitions high at first. The techniques of free weight exercises can then be taught using light loadings. Athletic exercises, such as power cleans, snatch, half squats and bench press, should be used with repetitions of greater than eight. Plyometric exercises, hopping and bounding activities, are also introduced at this stage.

Strength training programmes for young people should emphasise exercises which work those muscle groups stabilising the hip/spine joint and adding stability to rotation of the spine. Loadings on the spine and knees should be kept low; weights should not be supported on the back and depth jumps should not be attempted before the age of sixteen. As young athletes are often motivated by weight training, a coach is required to keep over enthusiasm in check and to encourage gradual progression.

Fig 60 Training for the developing athlete should feature a variety of
different methods.

AVOIDING INJURY

Many young people run too many miles in training, thus risking over-use injuries. Concern regarding over-use injuries and young runners has increased noticeably in recent years as a result of the increased popularity of mass participation events. These injuries are usually connected with the bones, which are the most vulnerable structure in young people. They include damage to the epiphyseal or growth plates of the long bones, inflammation of or damage to the point at which a tendon is attached to the bone, the apophysis, and stress fractures of bones in the lower limbs.

These injuries can be avoided by adopting a sensible approach to training and by not allowing young runners to undertake the training programmes of adults. Young people should not be allowed to train if they are experiencing pain and should be advised to see a sports doctor. The mileage of young athletes should be kept low and should only be increased by 7 to 10 miles per year. A guideline on mileage for runners in the foundation and developmental periods is provided below. Only training shoes with good shock absorbing qualities should be used, and when changing from hard to soft training surfaces or vice versa the training intensity should be reduced slightly. Training should feature a variety of methods and should not be limited to long, slow continuous miles.

Foundation Period

Limited to max of 2 × 20 min runs/week

Developmental Period

Age	Club Athlete	Elite 800/1,500	Elite 3,000/5,000
13	10–15		
14	10–15	15–20	
15	10–20	15–20	20–25
16	20	25–30	30–40
17	25	30 40	40 50
18	30	40 50	50 60

7 The Female Endurance Runner

It is only in recent years that endurance running has become an accepted sport for women. The 3,000m and marathon, after all, were only introduced to the programme of events for the Olympic Games in Los Angeles, 1984. Prior to that, the longest distance a woman could run in the Olympic Games was 1,500m and this event was only added to the Olympic programme in 1972.

Women's events were reluctantly included in the Olympics for the first time in 1928 at the Amsterdam Games, the longest event being the 800m which was won by Lina Radke of Germany in 2 minutes 16.8 seconds. Unfortunately, few of the competitors had ever tried the distance before and, as a result, they finished the race in considerable distress. The scene of several women collapsing with exhaustion at the finish of the race led to an outcry from the Press, who complained of the folly of women running so far. The outcome of these complaints was the removal of the 800m from the Olympic programme for thirty-two years. It wasn't until 1960 that the 800m was reintroduced and it was another twelve years before the 1,500m was introduced. The introduction of the 3,000m showed that it was slowly becoming accepted that women could take part in endurance running events, but had it not been for the growth of the mass participation marathons and the equal opportunities lobby we would still have been waiting today to see women running the marathon at the Olympic Games.

Although attitudes towards women taking part in endurance running events have gradually changed, there is still a lingering notion that women are not as suited to endurance running as their male counterparts. This is often evident in the approach of some female endurance runners and their coaches towards training. Women now take part in events from 800m to the marathon and beyond, yet there are still those who think that women cannot train as hard as men. This just isn't true, women *can* train as hard as men.

Female runners may not run as fast or complete the same volume of training as their male counterparts, but when it comes to effort and time spent in training their contributions are similar. Although it is a fact that there are performance-related differences between the genders, these do not extend to the amount of hard work that needs to be done to be a successful endurance athlete, as this component is the same for both sexes.

MALE/FEMALE DIFFERENCES

There are a number of structural, anatomical and physiological differences between the sexes which lead to performance variations in the endurance events. Despite these differences there are as many similarities, which explains the considerable

Fig 61 As attitudes towards women taking part in endurance running events have changed, more women have taken up the challenge of mass participation runs

overlap between the ranges of performance in men and women. Even though the best male endurance runners are faster than the best female runners, the best women run much faster than most men.

Performance differences between male and female runners can be explained by the influence of structural, anatomical and physiological factors on aerobic endurance and strength.

Aerobic Endurance

Maximal oxygen uptake considered as an absolute value (before being divided by the athlete's bodyweight) is substantially lower in women than in men. Absolute VO_2max for the average female is only 40 to 60 per cent of that of the average male. When bodyweight is taken into consideration and the relative value is calculated the difference is reduced to 20 to 30 per cent of that of the average male — much of the difference in absolute VO_2max being due to the female's smaller physique. If VO_2max is compared with lean body mass, and the body's stores of adipose tissue are ignored, the difference is further reduced to 15 per cent. This shows that the lower relative maximum oxygen uptake is partly due to the higher percentage of body fat in female runners. The percentage body fat in men in the general population ranges from 10.9 to 22.3 per cent, and for women the range is 21.9 to 29.8 per cent. Male endurance runners are often measured as having less than 10 per cent body fat, whilst percentages for female runners tend to be around 10 to 13 per cent. Top marathon runner Grete Waitz was measured at 9 per cent body fat on one occasion.

One factor which influences VO_2max is the blood's ability to transport oxygen around the body. Haemoglobin, which is contained in the red blood cells, carries the oxygen from the lungs to the muscles. The average male has about 6 per cent more red blood cells than the average female and also has 10 to 15 per cent more haemoglobin. A pint of blood from a woman will not have the potential to carry as much oxygen as a pint of blood from a man. However, it is thought that there are higher concentrations of 2,3 DPG in the haemoglobin of women which will partly offset the lower haemoglobin concentration (2, 3 diphosphoglycerate, present in the red blood cells, attaches itself to haemoglobin and encourages it to release oxygen). The lower haemoglobin and the fact that women have a lower total volume of blood, explain why women have a lower oxygen carrying potential.

Another important factor influencing VO_2max is the rate at which blood is pumped round the body. This is determined by the athlete's cardiac output, which is the product of the working heart rate and the heart's stroke volume. There is

no difference between working heart rates in men and women, so any difference in cardiac output is due to stroke volume. Men have on average an absolute cardiac output which is 40 per cent larger than that of women. When bodyweight is taken into consideration, the female has a cardiac output which is 80 to 90 per cent that of the male.

The ability of the muscles to extract oxygen from the bloodstream is a third factor which influences maximal oxygen uptake. Oxygen is extracted from the blood by myoglobin and is utilised in cells called mitochondria. The amount of myoglobin and number of mitochondria are lower in women than in men, and the density of oxidative enzymes in the female's mitochondria is also lower. This reduces the female's ability to extract oxygen and, together with their lower oxygen transporting capacity, contributes to the 15 per cent difference in maximal oxygen uptake between the sexes.

Maximum oxygen uptake is an important factor in endurance events. However, the longer the event, the more important the anaerobic threshold. When expressed as a percentage of VO_2max, there is no difference in anaerobic threshold between the sexes. However, the female runner has a lower VO_2max and therefore she has a lower absolute anaerobic threshold.

Strength

Strength levels in women are lower by 55 to 80 per cent than in men, due partly to women possessing less muscle mass. Muscle only accounts for 35.8 per cent of total bodyweight in women, compared with 41.8 per cent in men. Whilst they have a lower muscle mass than men, women have the same number of muscle fibres. They

Fig 62 Even though the best male endurance runners are faster than the best female runners, the best women run much faster than most men.

are of a smaller cross-sectional area, however, due to the lower plasma testosterone levels, the hormone which encourages muscle hypertrophy. Training will produce similar relative strength gains in men and women, but women will not increase total bodyweight significantly, as there will be considerably less muscle hypertrophy.

The lower strength levels of women influence performance in endurance events by preventing the development of an economical running action and the ability to sprint or change pace. Strength can be improved through training without the worry of increasing muscle mass.

Anaerobic Endurance

When it comes to the anaerobic energy systems, there are no differences between the sexes. The effects of anaerobic training and the acquired ability to tolerate the build-up of lactic acid are not sex dependent. There may, however, be some variation in lactate production during the menstrual cycle with improved anaerobic performance during the luteal phase.

Running Efficiency

The energy costs of running at set speeds may be higher in female athletes due to a reduced running efficiency caused by the female structure. Differences in the female anatomy also mean a lesser ability to sprint and change pace. The average female is smaller by about 5 inches and lighter by about 30 to 40 pounds than the average male. She has about 10 per cent more body fat, much of which is deposited around the thighs and buttocks lowering her centre of gravity. The wider pelvis, sloping of the thighs towards the knees, narrower shoulders, and shorter limbs in relation to body length all influence the running mechanics of women.

Whilst a woman's lower level of functional strength will have a negative influence on the development of sprinting speed, her better mobility and co-ordination levels are positive factors.

REPRODUCTIVE FUNCTION

Endurance training is associated with a number of changes which can occur in the menstrual cycle of female runners. Young female runners who engage in serious endurance training and are likely to develop a long, lithe figure may have their menarche delayed until their late teens. The female who takes up serious endurance training in her early twenties may experience exercise-induced secondary amenorrhea. Women taking up running after ovulation is well established will probably experience regular menses but may experience fewer pre-menstrual symptoms than usual. These changes are associated with lower basal oestrogen levels and are reversible when training ceases.

Like most women who wish to control their fertility, the female runner may need to consider birth control methods. Whilst the birth control pill is a convenient form of contraception, it is not popular amongst endurance runners. Although there are a number of positive aspects associated with the pill, including the predictable menstrual cycle, there are negative aspects which may affect performance. Female endurance runners using the pill have experienced a significant reduction in their maximum oxygen uptake. This and the possibility of increased bodyweight will result in a decrease in relative VO_2max. After ceasing

Fig 63   The energy costs of women running may be higher than those
of men.

use of the birth control pill VO_2max should return to normal values within six weeks.

As intra-uterine devices are not popular with athletic women, and as changes in the menstrual cycle due to endurance training make the rhythm method even more un-reliable, barrier methods may be the most practical solution to birth control for the endurance athlete.

During menstruation haemoglobin levels may fall leaving the female athlete anaemic. Normal haemoglobin concentra-tion tests may show the athlete to be below normal levels, but this could be due to the increased blood volume caused by train-ing. To check if the female athlete is anaemic it is important to measure serum ferritin levels which correlate with the body's total iron stores.

TRAINING IMPLICATIONS

If women wish to reach the highest levels of participation, they must be prepared to spend the same amount of time in training as elite men would. Their training loads will be at the same intensity and involve a similar volume of training to those of men with equivalent best performances. Any difference in training loads will be related to performance level rather than gender. The methods used in training and the annual training plans are the same as those for men. Within the annual training plan, more attention may be devoted to the develop-ment of aerobic endurance and strength, as women are weaker in these areas of conditioning. However, this should not detract from other important aspects of training.

Women may need to supplement iron and vitamin C as they are prone to anaemia at certain stages of the menstrual cycle. A doctor with an interest in sport should be asked to monitor haemoglobin levels and to prescribe iron therapy if required. It may also be advisable to supplement the B-complex vitamins, which are involved in energy metabolism, especially if the runner is using oral contraceptives. Some runners and the parents of young female runners may be concerned at the loss of menstrual periods associated with endurance train-ing. In such cases, the runner should consult her doctor who may refer her to a specialist, who, in turn, can conduct tests to confirm that the loss of periods is due to the training load and will be restored when training ceases.

Some female runners tend to worry about their weight and are not always sensible in weight control practices. It may be neces-sary to recruit the services of a dietician who can advise on diet and weight control. Percentage body fat and weight are useful measures to keep throughout the training year to help ensure that the runner reaches her optimal relative maximum oxygen uptake.

8 Nutrition for Runners

The food and drink which a runner consumes not only supplies the carbohydrate and fat, which provide the energy needed for competition and training, but also contains nutrients which aid recovery and ensure the metabolic processes function properly. The nutrients in our food are:

1. Carbohydrate – the body's preferred source of energy.
2. Fats – another source of energy and a carrier of certain vitamins.
3. Protein – essential for growth, repair of tissues and metabolism.
4. Vitamins – essential for the body's metabolism.
5. Minerals – essential for the body's metabolism.
6. Water – as 60 per cent of the body is water this needs to be replaced regularly.
7. Fibre – essential for the health of the digestive system.

Runners need a diet containing a variety of foods which provide the nutrients essential not just for running but also for good health. The importance of each of the nutrients to the runner can be seen as we examine them in detail. Simple changes to dietary habits are recommended, which, if followed, should ensure that the runner eats the right types and quantities of food.

It shouldn't be assumed that the majority of runners eat a healthy diet. If the diet of the general population is anything to go by, they probably don't. The United Kingdom has a poor record of heart disease in comparison to other nations, and that has been partly attributed to diet. Many people consume too much fat, sugar and salt and not enough fibre in their diets. Diets which are unhealthy for the general population are also inappropriate for the runner.

Before considering changes which may be required in the eating habits of runners to ensure an appropriate diet, we should consider each of the different nutrients, their importance to the runner and the foods in which they can be found.

NUTRIENTS

Carbohydrate

Carbohydrate is the major source of energy for most running events. It is really only in the marathon and other long distance events that the runner uses fat as a main source of energy. Carbohydrate comes in two forms, starch or sugar, which are both converted into muscle glycogen to be used in the muscles to provide energy. Each gram of carbohydrate will produce 4 calories of energy and in the process will use 0.7 litres of oxygen. The store of this fuel in the body will last for about 100 minutes of running at a steady pace.

Although sugars (for example sweets, sugar, lemonade) and starches (for example bread, pasta, fruit, vegetables) produce the same amount of energy, starches are the preferred forms of carbohydrate for athletic performance, as they are accompanied by vitamins and minerals. These vitamins and minerals are missing in sugary

Fig 64   *Kirsty Wade, Commonwealth Games 800m and 1,500m Champion 1986, is an athlete who is known to pursue a policy of healthy eating.*

foods which are often referred to as 'empty calorie foods'.

Fats

Fats are the body's long term source of energy and are used along with carbohydrate when the body performs low intensity work, thus sparing the stores of carbohydrate. If the body starts to run low on carbohydrate, it will increase its use of fats. There is such a large store of fat that it could provide energy for several days, unlike the store of carbohydrate which would last less than two hours. Stored fats are converted into 'free fatty acids', which are used in the muscle to provide energy. A gram of fat produces 9 calories of energy at a cost of 2.03 litres of oxygen. So even though fats produce more than twice as much energy per gram as carbohydrate, the oxygen cost of producing the energy is much higher:

Fuel	Energy produced	Oxygen cost	Oxygen/ cal
Carbohydrate	4 cal	0.7l/m	0.175l
Fats	9 cal	2.03l/m	0.225l

Fats also provide the body with insulation, protect vital organs, supply certain vitamins and make food appetising and filling. Too much fat in the diet, however, can lead to health problems including heart disease. For better health, vegetable or polyunsaturated fats are preferred to animal or saturated fats.

Protein

Protein is involved in growth and the repair of damaged tissue. It also has a role in the metabolic process that converts both carbohydrate and fats into energy and in helping the body to tolerate the build-up of lactic acid produced during anaerobic activity. The average person needs 1–2 grams of protein per kilogram of their bodyweight each day. Athletes in strength related events, who need to build muscle bulk, may need up to 4 grams per kilogram of their bodyweight. Some strength athletes take protein in powder form to supplement their diets. It is generally agreed, however, that this is not necessary as most diets provide more than 4 grams per kilogram of bodyweight per day, and such a practice is certainly not suitable for runners who are not concerned in building muscle bulk.

Protein in the food we eat is broken down into amino acids. There are 25 known amino acids, 8 of which cannot be manufactured in the body and have to be found in our food. Protein can be found in either animal or vegetable sources. Animal sources, such as meat, fish, eggs or dairy products, are often referred to as complete protein foods, as they contain all of the 8 essential amino acids. Vegetable sources are described as being incomplete as they lack or are low in at least one of the essential amino acids. Vegetarians argue that all of these amino acids can be gained from vegetable sources by combining different types of vegetable.

Foodstuff	% Quality of protein	% Concen- tration	
Eggs	100	12	
Milk	94	3.5	Animal
Beef	83	17	source
Fish	70	16	
Soya	73	7	Vege-
Rice	83	7	table
Potato	90	2	source

Vitamins

Vitamins are essential as they allow our bodies to function properly, contributing to the various chemical processes which regulate metabolism, release energy and repair tissue. These vitamins are either 'water soluble' or 'fat soluble' in nature.

Water Soluble Vitamins

Vitamin	Role	Source
C	Fights infection and is involved in iron, protein and energy metabolism	Fresh fruit, vegetables
B1 (Thiamine)	Energy metabolism and nervous system	Brown bread, milk, vegetables, potatoes, meat, pulses, eggs, cheese, fish, fowl
B2 (Riboflavine)	Energy and protein metabolism	Milk and milk products, brown bread, meat, fish, green vegetables, eggs
B6 (Pyridoxine)	Protein metabolism	Bread, milk, eggs, vegetables, nuts, meat, fish, fowl
B12	Red blood cell production, nervous system, energy and protein metabolism	Meat, liver, milk, eggs
B3 (Niacin)	Energy metabolism, free fatty acid production	Brown bread, meat, fish, fowl, peanuts
Folic acid	Blood cell production, growth, protein metabolism	Liver, raw green vegetables, pulses

Fat Soluble Vitamins

Vitamin	Role	Source
A	Growth, repair, eyes, skin, fights infection, possibly aids energy production	Margarine, butter, milk, liver, carrots, egg yolk
D	Calcium – bone formation	Sunshine, margarine, butter, egg yolk, fish oil
E	Protects vitamins and essential free fatty acids	Wheatgerm, egg, vegetable oil
K	Blood clotting	Green vegetables

Water soluble vitamins have an important role in energy and protein metabolism and they are thought to be depleted as a result of strenuous training. It is therefore important that foods rich in such vitamins are selected by athletes in preference to the so-called 'empty calorie' foods; so starches should be chosen instead of sugars. These vitamins are also easily destroyed in processing and cooking – a good reason for including fresh fruit and vegetables in the diet and for avoiding the overcooking of vegetables.

If there are adequate amounts of vitamins in the athlete's diet, supplementation should not be necessary. However, it may be appropriate for endurance runners to supplement B and C, the water soluble vitamins, which can be supplemented safely. There are hazards, however, in supplementing the fat soluble vitamins and the athlete's intake of vitamins A, D, E and K should come from his diet rather than from vitamin preparations.

Minerals

Like vitamins, minerals have an important role in the body's metabolic processes. The minerals, their importance and sources are:

Sodium from its main source, common salt, is plentiful in most foods and in the salt-cellars on most tables. It is generally accepted that for better health we should cut down in our consumption of table salt.

It is common for runners to supplement iron. Care needs to be taken when doing so, as with the fat soluble vitamins, for the body cannot get rid of excess iron and too much can lead to a toxic condition. It is recommended that iron supplements are taken only on the advice of a medical expert.

Water

Of all the nutrients, water is the most important as it would not be possible to survive long without it. The body needs a regular supply to function normally. Water is needed to carry nutrients and to regulate body temperature. During long competitions or in hot conditions, we often lose too much water and become dehydrated. This stops our body functioning effectively and can lead to heat related stress problems. Runners have to drink lots of fluid, especially during long races or in hot environments.

Vitamin	Role	Source
Iron	Oxygen transport	Brown bread, meat, vegetables, pulses
Calcium	Bone formation and muscle enzyme activity	Milk, milk products, cheese, vegetables, bread
Sodium	Fluid regulation and salt/water balance	Most foods, kitchen salt
Potassium	General constitution	Vegetables, fruit, potatoes
Magnesium	Stimulus transfer in muscle	Green vegetables, nuts, pulses, fruit
Phosphorus	Bone formation	Milk products, vegetables, bread

Fibre

Fibre is essential in the diet to ensure the proper health of our digestive system. Many highly processed foods have the fibre removed, so it is necessary to include foods such as wholemeal bread in our diets.

A SUITABLE DIET

Having considered the importance of each of the seven types of nutrients to running performance, and having noted the types of foods that provide them, we need to compare the proportions of the nutrients in the average diet with those of the ideal diet for participation in training.

The diet of the average person in the United Kingdom contains the following percentages of nutrients:

Protein	11%
Fats	38%
Carbohydrate	45% (Sugar 20%)
	(Starch 25%)
Fibre	20grams/day
Salt	10grams/day

Nutritionists are recommending that changes be made to the above diet to make it more healthy. They have suggested the following, which is the type of diet that is appropriate for the runner.

Protein	11%
Fats	25–30%
Carbohydrate	55–60% (Sugar 10%)
	(Starch 45–50%)
Fibre	30grams/day
Salt	5grams/day

The majority of runners have diets which are similar to those of the general population. If they are to alter the nutritional balance of their diets to that recommended for better health, runners will have to make the following changes:

1. Runners should choose a diet containing a variety of foods.
2. Runners' carbohydrate consumption should be at least 55 per cent of their total energy intake.
3. Runners' sugar consumption should only be one quarter of their total carbohydrate intake.
4. Runners' fat intake should only be 30 per cent of their total energy consumption.
5. Runners' saturated fat consumption should be reduced to one third of the total fat intake by substitution of polyunsaturated fats.
6. Runners' cholesterol intake should be less than 300mg/day.
7. Runners' salt intake should be reduced to about 5g/day.
8. Runners' intake of cereals, fruits and vegetables should be increased.

To effect these changes to the runners' diet the following steps can be taken. Adopting the recommendations below will alter eating habits, changing the intake of nutrients, and moving towards a diet promoting better health and athletic performance.

1. Use natural vegetable cooking oils and try grilled food in preference to fried food.
2. Buy cooking oils and margarines marked as high in polyunsaturates. Spread butter or margarine thinly. Don't put butter on vegetables.
3. Eat no more than three to four eggs per week.

4. If you eat red meat, select lean cuts and trim fat before cooking. Cut down on beef, lamb and pork, and eat more poultry and fish instead. Cut down on processed and tinned meats, sausages and meat pies.

5. Eat more bread, about six slices per day, and preferably wholemeal rather than white.

6. Use less salt in cooking and don't use extra salt on the meal.

7. Cut down on sugar in tea, coffee and on breakfast cereals. Choose breakfast cereals that are not pre-coated with sugar.

8. Substitute skimmed or semi-skimmed milk for whole milk.

9. Choose low fat dairy products when selecting cheese or yoghurt.

10. Cut down on sweet cakes, puddings, biscuits, jam, etc. Try fresh fruit, dried fruit, nuts, tea-cakes and scones, or a sandwich instead.

11. Drink pure fruit juices in preference to lemonade or concentrates.

12. Eat more vegetables and salads of all kinds including potatoes and beans. Cook green vegetables for shorter periods of time in less water.

13. Eat more fresh fruit, fresh fruit salads and nuts.

14. Eat more cereal foods, such as wholemeal pasta and rice.

NUTRITION FOR COMPETITION

So far we have discussed the everyday nutrition of the runner and have not considered nutrition in relation to competition. There are important nutritional rules for the pre-competition and post-competition phases, in addition to nutrition during competition itself.

Pre-competition

Three to four days before competition, it is important to take steps to ensure that the body's glycogen stores are high. Demanding training sessions which lead to the depletion of muscle glycogen are dropped from the training programme in preference for light training. A good quality high carbohydrate diet should be followed to ensure that glycogen levels are not just brought up to normal levels but are, in fact, enhanced.

Marathon runners tend to undertake a regime aimed at increasing the body's stores of carbohydrate so that less fat needs to be used for energy during the event. The traditional carbohydrate loading regime features the following stages (it assumes the marathon takes place on a Saturday afternoon):

1. Seven days prior to the race, the marathon runner undertakes a long run of about twenty miles in order to deplete his muscle glycogen stores (Sunday morning).

2. For the next three days the marathon runner follows a high protein, low carbohydrate diet (Sunday lunch to Wednesday lunch).

3. This is then replaced by a high carbohydrate diet from lunchtime three days before the marathon (Wednesday lunch to Saturday lunch).

Although in theory this system will more than double the normal muscle glycogen stores, it can have a number of drawbacks. Some runners are unhappy with a run of twenty miles so close to the race, and some find training on the low carbohydrate diet stressful. The low carbohydrate diet often causes diarrhoea, which can drain the runner both mentally and physically and

Fig 65   In long distance races such as the marathon, nutrition plays an important part in both the preparation and the competition itself.

produces a dehydrated state. Sleep may be affected, and an attitude of not feeling well or not being prepared is often created. As no one wants to go to the start line lacking in confidence, it is important that the negative aspects of the diet are avoided.

There are two alternatives to this traditional diet and both involve increased carbohydrate intake for three to four days prior to the race. The only difference between the two is that in one the training loads during the last week are kept low, whilst in the other a hard training session is carried out four days before the race. Both methods will increase the body's stores of muscle glycogen, the latter being slightly better than the former. Whichever method is to be used, it is best to try them out during the training period rather than chance using an untried method during an important marathon.

One of the results of carbohydrate loading is an increase in bodyweight. Carbohydrate is stored in the body with water and this increase in body fluid leads to an increase in weight. As the body loses fluid during endurance running events, these additional stores caused by the carbohydrate loading may be an advantage.

Competition Nutrition

Carbohydrate loading continues till the last meal before the race. The pre-competition meal should be light and easily digestible, and should be taken three to four hours before the race to allow for digestion. A high carbohydrate drink can be taken by those who find it difficult to eat on the day of a marathon but this should be taken one to one and a half hours in advance of the competition. The drink should include a mixture of quick and slow absorbable carbohydrates. In long distance events and in hot, humid climates water should be sipped right up to the start of the race. Drinking two cups of coffee prior to the start of a long distance race may be beneficial as the caffeine encourages fat utilisation and may help to spare carbohydrate stores. Caffeine is a banned drug, but this applies to large quantities of the substance and not to the small amount which the body takes in when drinking tea, coffee or a soft drink.

During long distance road races of more than ten kilometres, refreshment, water and sponge stations are provided. Water stations are provided every five kilometres and it is recommended that runners drink at each of them. Dehydration can lead to heat stress problems, especially if the race takes place in a hot or humid environment, so it is important to replace the fluid lost through sweating. Prior to the start of the race, the runner should drink about half a pint of cold water during the half-hour before the race starts. This will keep the runner going to the first station. Drinking on the run is not easy and should be practised during a training run involving laps round a course which passes your home or some other convenient place. Place your paper cups or drink-bottles on the garden wall and practise picking up a container and drinking from it, without stopping, each time you complete a lap.

It is also recommended that you use the sponges provided between the refreshment stations. Do not drink the water, as it is possible that the sponge has been used before. Instead, squeeze water over your head and over your thighs.

You can provide your own drinks in some marathons, but this is obviously difficult in a mass participation event. Personal drinks usually contain some carbohydrate and electrolytes. These can be made up, or the runner can use one of the many commercial preparations.

In events like the 800m and the 1,500m, it is common in championships to have a number of rounds on the same day. The runner will want to eat between rounds. Food should be kept light and should be of the good quality carbohydrate type. A drink which contains both carbohydrate and minerals would be suitable between rounds when the runner finds it difficult to consume food.

Post-competition

A carbohydrate drink, which will help to replace depleted glycogen stores, can be taken within ten minutes of the event being completed. It is also possible to do this after each training session. The first meal should be taken an hour and a half to two hours after the competition and should contain carbohydrate, protein, vitamins and minerals. Orange juice or tomato juice is useful in helping to replace minerals lost, in particular in the longer events.

Appendix

MEN'S WORLD RECORDS

800m

1:51.9 Ted Meredith (USA) 1912
1:51.6 Otto Peltzer (Germany) 1926
1:50.6 Seraphin Martin (France) 1928
1:49.8 Thomas Hampson (GB) 1932
    (actual time 1:49.7)
1:49.8 Ben Eastman (USA) 1934
1:49.7 Glenn Cunningham (USA) 1936
1:49.6 Elroy Robinson (USA) 1937
1:48.4 Sidney Wooderson (GB) 1938
1:46.6 Rudolf Harbig (Germany) 1939
1:45.7 Roger Moens (Belgium) 1955
1:44.3 Peter Snell (NZ) 1962
1:44.3 Ralph Doubell (Australia) 1968
1:44.3 David Wottle (USA) 1972
1:43.7 Marcello Fiasconaro (Italy) 1973
1:43.5 Alberto Juantorena (Cuba) 1976
1:43.44 Alberto Juantorena (Cuba) 1977
1:42.33 Sebastian Coe (GB) 1979
1:41.73 Sebastian Coe (GB) 1981

1,500m

3:55.8 Abel Kiviat (USA) 1912
3:54.7 John Zander (Sweden) 1917
3:52.6 Paavo Nurmi (Finland) 1924
3:51.0 Otto Peltzer (Germany) 1926
3:49.2 Jules Ladoumegue (France) 1930
3:49.2 Luigi Beccali (Italy) 1933
3:49.0 Luigi Beccali (Italy) 1933
3:48.8 Bill Bonthron (USA) 1934
3:47.8 Jack Lovelock (NZ) 1936
3:47.6 Gundar Hägg (Sweden) 1941
3:45.8 Gundar Hägg (Sweden) 1942
3:45.0 Arne Andersson (Sweden) 1943
3:43.0 Gundar Hägg (Sweden) 1944
3:43.0 Lennart Strand (Sweden) 1947
3:43.0 Werner Lueg (Germany) 1952
3:42.8 Wes Santee (USA) 1954

3:41.8 John Landy (Australia) 1954
3:40.8 Sandor Iharos (Hungary) 1955
3:40.8 Laszlo Tabori (Hungary) 1955
3:40.6 Istvan Rozsavolgyi (Hungary) 1956
3:40.2 Olavi Salonen (Finland) 1957
3:40.2 Olavi Salsola (Finland) 1957
3:38.1 Stanislav Jungwirth
    (Czechoslovakia) 1957
3:36.0 Herb Elliott (Australia) 1958
3:35.6 Herb Elliott (Australia) 1960
3:33.1 Jim Ryun (USA) 1967
3:32.2 Filbert Bayi (Tanzania) 1974
3:32.12 Sebastian Coe (GB) 1979
3:32.09 Steve Ovett (GB) 1980
3:31.36 Steve Ovett (GB) 1980
3:31.24 Sydney Maree (USA) 1983
3:30.77 Steve Ovett (GB) 1983
3:29.67 Steve Cram (GB) 1985
3:29.46 Said Aouita (Morroco) 1985

Mile

4:14.4 John Paul Jones (USA) 1913
4:12.6 Norman Taber (USA) 1915
4:10.4 Paavo Nurmi (Finland) 1923
4:09.2 Jules Ladoumegue (France) 1931
4:07.6 Jack Lovelock (NZ) 1933
4:06.8 Glenn Cunningham (USA) 1934
4:06.4 Sidney Wooderson (GB) 1937
4:06.2 Gundar Hägg (Sweden) 1942
4:06.2 Arne Andersson (Sweden) 1942
4:04.6 Gundar Hägg (Sweden) 1942
4:02.6 Arne Andersson (Sweden) 1943
4:01.6 Arne Andersson (Sweden) 1944
4:01.4 Gundar Hägg (Sweden) 1945
    (actual time 4:01.3)
3:59.4 Roger Bannister (GB) 1954
3:58.0 John Landy (Australia) 1954
    (actual time 3:57.9)
3:57.2 Derek Ibbotson (GB) 1957
3:54.5 Herb Elliott (Australia) 1958
3:54.4 Peter Snell (NZ) 1962
3:54.1 Peter Snell (NZ) 1964
3:53.6 Michel Jazy (France) 1965

3:51.3 Jim Ryun (USA) 1966
3:51.1 Jim Ryun (USA) 1967
3:51.0 Filbert Bayi (Tanzania) 1975
3:49.4 John Walker (NZ) 1975
3:49.0 Sebastian Coe (GB) 1979
3:48.8 Steve Ovett (GB) 1980
3:48.53 Sebastian Coe (GB) 1981
3:48.4 Steve Ovett (GB) 1981
3:47.33 Sebastian Coe (GB) 1981
3:46.32 Steve Cram (GB) 1985

5,000m

14:36.6 Hannes Kolehmainen (Finland) 1912
14:35.4 Paavo Nurmi (Finland) 1922
14:28.2 Paavo Nurmi (Finland) 1924
14:17.0 Lauri Lehtinen (Finland) 1932
14:08.8 Taisto Máki (Finland) 1939
13:58.2 Gundar Hägg (Sweden) 1942
13:57.2 Emil Zátopek (Czechoslovakia) 1954
13:56.6 Vladimir Kuts (USSR) 1954
13:51.6 Chris Chataway (GB) 1954
13:51.2 Vladimir Kuts (USSR) 1954
13:50.8 Sándor Iharos (Hungary) 1955
13:46.8 Vladimir Kuts (USSR) 1955
13:40.6 Sándor Iharos (Hungary) 1955
13:36.8 Gordon Pirie (GB) 1956
13:35.0 Vladimir Kuts (USSR) 1957
13:34.8 Ron Clarke (Australia) 1965
13:33.6 Ron Clarke (Australia) 1965
13:25.8 Ron Clarke (Australia) 1965
13:24.2 Kipchoge Keino (Kenya) 1965
13:16.6 Ron Clarke (Australia) 1966
13:16.4 Lasse Viren (Finland) 1972
13:13.0 Emiel Puttemans (Belgium) 1972
13:12.9 Dick Quax (NZ) 1977
13:08.4 Henry Rono (Kenya) 1978
13:06.20 Henry Rono (Kenya) 1981
13:00.41 Dave Moorcroft (GB) 1982
13:00.40 Said Aouita (Morocco) 1985

10,000m

30:58.8 Jean Bouin (France) 1911
30:40.2 Paavo Nurmi (Finland) 1921
30:35.4 Ville Ritola (Finland) 1924
30:23.2 Ville Ritola (Finland) 1924
30:06.2 Paavo Nurmi (Finland) 1924
30:05.6 Ilmari Salminen (Finland) 1937
30:02.0 Taisto Maki (Finland) 1938
29:52.6 Taisto Maki (Finland) 1939

29:35.4 Viljo Heino (Finland) 1944
29:28.4 Emil Zátopek (Czechoslovakia) 1949
29:27.2 Viljo Heino (Finland) 1949
29:21.2 Emil Zátopek (Czechoslovakia) 1949
29:02.6 Emil Zátopek (Czechoslovakia) 1950
29:01.6 Emil Zátopek (Czechoslovakia) 1953
28:54.2 Emil Zátopek (Czecholslovakia) 1954
28:42.8 Sandor Iharos (Hungary) 1956
28:30.4 Vladimir Kuts (USSR) 1956
28:18.8 Pyotr Bolotnikov (USSR) 1960
28:18.2 Pyotr Bolotnikov (USSR) 1962
28:15.6 Ron Clarke (Australia) 1963
27:39.4 Ron Clarke (Australia) 1965
27:38.4 Lasse Viren (Finland) 1972
27:30.8 Dave Bedford (GB) 1973
27:30.5 Samson Kimobwa (Kenya) 1977
27:22.4 Henry Rono (Kenya) 1978
27:13.81 Fernando Mamede (Portugal) 1984

3,000m Steeplechase

8:49.6 Sandor Rozsnyoi (Hungary) 1954
8:47.8 Pentti Karvonen (Finland) 1955
8:45.4 Pentti Karvonen (Finland) 1955
8:45.4 Vasili Vlasenko (USSR) 1955
8:41.2 Jerzy Chromik (Poland) 1955
8:40.2 Jerzy Chromik (Poland) 1955
8:39.8 Semyon Rzhishchin (USSR) 1956
8:35.6 Sandor Rozsnyoi (Hungary) 1956
8:35.6 Semyon Rzhishchin (USSR) 1958
8:32.0 Jerzy Chromik (Poland) 1958
8:31.4 Zdzislaw Krzyszkowiak (Poland) 1960
8:31.2 Grigori Taran (USSR) 1961
8:30.4 Zdzislaw Krzyszkowiak (Poland) 1961
8:29.6 Gaston Roelants (Belgium) 1963
8:26.4 Gaston Roelants (Belgium) 1965
8:24.2 Jouko Kuha (Finland) 1968
8:22.2 Vladimir Dudin (USSR) 1969
8:22.0 Kerry O'Brien (Australia) 1970
8:20.8 Anders Gärderud (Sweden) 1972
8:19.8 Benjamin Jipcho (Kenya) 1973
8:14.0 Benjamin Jipcho (Kenya) 1973
8:10.4 Anders Gärderud (Sweden) 1975
8:09.8 Anders Gärderud (Sweden) 1975
8:08.0 Anders Gärderud (Sweden) 1976
8:05.4 Henry Rono (Kenya) 1978

Marathon

2:55:18.4 John Hayes (USA) 1908
2:52:45.4 Robert Fowler (USA) 1909

2:46:52.6 James Clark (USA) 1909
2:46:04.6 Albert Raines (USA) 1909
2:42:31 Harry Barrett (GB) 1913
2:36:06.6 Alexis Ahlgren (Sweden) 1913
2:32:35.8 Johannes Kolehmainen
       (Finland) 1920
2:29:01.8 Albert Michelsen (USA) 1925
2:27:49 Fusashige Suzuki (Japan) 1935
2:26:44 Yasuo Ikenaka (Japan) 1935
2:26:42 Kitei Son (Japan) 1935
2:25:39 Yun Bok Suh (Korea) 1947
2:20:42.2 Jim Peters (GB) 1952
2:18:40.2 Jim Peters (GB) 1953
2:18:34.8 Jim Peters (GB) 1953
2:17:39.4 Jim Peters (GB) 1954
2:15:17 Sergey Popov (USSR) 1958
2:15:16.2 Abebe Bikila (Ethiopia) 1960
2:15:15.8 Toru Terasawa (Japan) 1963
2:14:28 Leonard Edelen (USA) 1963
2:13:55 Basil Heatley (GB) 1964
2:12:11.2 Abebe Bikila (Ethiopia) 1964
2:12:00 Morio Shigematsu (Japan) 1965
2:09:36.4 Derek Clayton (Australia) 1967
2:08:33.6 Derek Clayton (Australia) 1969
2:08:12.7 Alberto Salazar (USA) 1981
       (found to be a short course)
2:08:18 Robert de Castella (Australia) 1981
2:08:05 Steve Jones (GB) 1984
2:07:11.6 Carlos Lopes (Portugal) 1985

WOMEN'S WORLD RECORDS

800m

2:16.8 Lina Batschauer-Radke
      (Germany) 1928
2:15.8 Anna Larsson (Sweden) 1944
2:14.8 Anna Larsson (Sweden) 1945
2:13.8 Anna Larsson (Sweden) 1945
2:13.0 Yedokiya Vasilyeva (USSR) 1950
2:12.2 Valentina Pomogayeva (USSR) 1951
2:12.0 Nina Pletnyova (USSR) 1951
2:08.5 Nina Pletnyova (USSR) 1952
2:07.3 Nina Otkalenko (USSR) 1953
2:06.6 Nina Otkalenko (USSR) 1954
2:05.0 Nina Otkalenko (USSR) 1955
2:04.3 Lyudmila Shevtsova (USSR) 1960
2:04.3 Lyudmila Shevtsova (USSR) 1960
2:01.2 Dixie Willis (Australia) 1962

2:01.1 Ann Packer (GB) 1964
2:01.0 Judy Pollock (Australia) 1967
2:00.5 Vera Nikolic (Yugoslavia) 1968
1:58.5 Hildegard Falck (FRG) 1971
1:57.5 Svetla Zlateva (Bulgaria) 1973
1:56.0 Valentina Gerasimova (USSR) 1976
1:54.9 Tatyana Kazankina (USSR) 1976
1:54.85 Nadyezhda Olizarenko (USSR) 1980
1:53.43 Nadyezhda Olizarenko (USSR) 1980
1:53.28 Jarmila Kratochvilova
      (Czechoslovakia) 1983

1,500m

4:17.3 Anne Smith (GB) 1967
4:15.6 Maria Gommers
      (The Netherlands) 1967
4:12.4 Paola Pigni (Italy) 1969
4:10.7 Jaroslava Jehlickova
      (Czechoslovakia) 1969
4:09.6 Karen Burneleit (GDR) 1971
4:06.9 Lyudmila Bragina (USSR) 1972
4:06.5 Lyudmila Bragina (USSR) 1972
4:05.1 Lyudmila Bragina (USSR) 1972
4:01.4 Lyudmila Bragina (USSR) 1972
3:56.0 Tatyana Kazankina (USSR) 1976
3:55.0 Tatyana Kazankina (USSR) 1980
3:52.47 Tatyana Kazankina (USSR) 1980

Mile

4:37.0 Anne Smith (GB) 1967
4:36.8 Maria Gommers
      (The Netherlands) 1969
4:35.3 Ellen Tittel (FRG) 1971
4:29.5 Paola Pigni-Cacchi (Italy) 1973
4:23.8 Natalia Marasescu (Romania) 1977
4:22.1 Natalia Marasescu (Romania) 1979
4:21.68 Mary Decker (USA) 1980
4:20.89 Liudmila Veselkova (USSR) 1981
4:17.44 Maricica Puica (Romania) 1982
4:16.71 Mary Slaney (USA) 1985

3,000m

8:52.8 Lyudmila Bragina (USSR) 1974
8:46.6 Grete Andersen (Norway) 1975
8:45.4 Grete Andersen-Waitz (Norway) 1976
8:27.12 Lyudmila Bragina (USSR) 1976
8:26.78 Svetlana Ulmasova (USSR) 1982
8:22.62 Tatyana Kazankina (USSR) 1984

10,000m

30:59.42 Ingrid Kristianson (Norway) 1985
30:13.74 Ingrid Kristianson (Norway) 1986

Marathon

3:27.45 Dale Greig (GB) 1964
3:19.33 Mildred Sampson (NZ) 1964
3:15.22 Maureen Wilton (Canada) 1967
3:07.26 Anni Pede-Erdkamp (FRG) 1967
3:02.53 Caroline Walker (USA) 1970
3:01.42 Elizabeth Bonner (USA) 1971
2:46.30 Adrienne Beames (Australia) 1971

2:46.24 Chantal Longlace (France) 1974
2:43:54.5 Jacqueline Hansen (USA) 1974
2:42.24 Liane Winter (FRG) 1975
2:40:15.8 Christa Vahlensieck (FRG) 1975
2:38.19 Jacqueline Hansen (USA) 1975
2:35:15.4 Chantal Langlace (France) 1977
2:34:47.5 Christa Vahlensieck (FRG) 1977
2:32:29.8 Grete Waitz (Norway) 1978
2:27:32.6 Grete Waitz (Norway) 1979
2:25:41.3 Grete Waitz (Norway) 1980
2:25.29 Allison Roe (NZ) 1981
        (found to be a short course)
2:25.29 Grete Waitz (Norway) 1982
2:22.43 Joan Benoit (USA) 1982
2:21.06 Ingrid Kristianson (Norway) 1985

Further Reading

BAAB publications

Brook, N. *Mobility Training* (1986)
Dick, F. W. *Training Theory* (1984)
Dick, F. W., Johnson, C. and Paish W. *Strength Training* (1978)
Watts, D. and Wilson, H. *Middle and Long Distance, Marathon and Steeplechase*

The above can be obtained from:

BAAB/AAA Publications Sales Centre
5 Church Road
Great Bookham
Leatherhead
Surrey

Other publications

Costill, D. *A Scientific Approach to Distance Running* (Tafnews Press, Los Altos, 1979)
Dick, F. W. *Sports Training Principles* (Lepus Books, London, 1980)
Humphreys, J. and Holman, R. *Focus on the Marathon* (E. P. Publishing, Wakefield, 1983)
Humphreys, J. and Holman, R. *Focus on Middle Distance Running* (E. P. Publishing, Wakefield, 1984)
Schmolinsky, G. *Track and Field* (Sportverlag Berlin, 1978)
Sharkey, B. J. *Physiology of Fitness* (Human Kinetics, Champaign, 1984)
Wells, C. L. *Women, Sport and Performance* (Human Kinetics, Champaign, 1985)

Useful Addresses

BAAB
Francis House
Francis Street
London
SW1P 1DL

IAAF
3 Hans Crescent
Knightsbridge
London
SW1X OLN

The Amateur Athletic Association and the
Womens' Amateur Athletic Association can
also be contacted at the above address.

Index

Index

Other Titles in The Skills of the Game Series

◆ Also available in paperback

Further details of titles available or in preparation can be obtained from the publishers.